MANAGING CHANGE

PRACTICAL POINTERS
KEY EXAMPLES

National Economic Development Office

Training Agency

This report has been prepared for publication
by the Manpower and Education Division of
the National Economic Development Office
(NEDO) in association with the Training
Agency.

NEDO is the independent office which supports
and assists the National Economic
Development Council (NEDC), its sector
groups and working parties.

The NEDC brings together representatives of
Government, management, the trade unions
and other interests to assess economic
performance and opportunities for improving
it.

The NEDC meets quarterly, under the
chairmanship of the Chancellor of the
Exchequer and other Secretaries of State.

NEDC sector groups work on practical
industrial issues in agriculture, tourism and
leisure, engineering, electronics, construction,
pharmaceuticals and textiles.

The National Economic Development Office
plays a key role in promoting change and the
ways in which obstacles to growth may be
overcome.

ISBN 0 7292 0965 2

Published by

National Economic Development Office
Millbank Tower
Millbank
London SW1P 4QX

September 1989

INTRODUCTION

THE CHALLENGE OF CHANGE

Change is inevitable; the techniques for managing change need to be understood and applied systematically.
Change can be managed if the environment is understood.
Managing change requires an increasingly wide and co-ordinated set of actions

These conclusions would have been drawn by those taking part in a conference in 1988 called The Challenge of Change. It was organised by the National Economic Development Office and the Training Agency to discuss a summary report of a research programme that had been commissioned to find out how companies which had successfully undergone major change had approached this task. It was addressed by senior managers from the companies involved in the research and by managers from organisations which had made major changes in recent years.

This report brings together the results of the research and the messages of the speakers of the Conference. It is arranged as follows:

Part One "Understanding the Nature of Change" describes the
increasing pressures for change and suggests that companies are adopting
a new approach.

This starts on page 5

Part Two "Making Change Happen" sets out, step by step, the full
range of initiatives which are available to companies that want to
transform their performance.

This starts on page 7

Part Three "A Case-book of Change" describes the process of
change in twelve companies and operating units in the UK, France
and the United States.

This starts on page 16

The Challenge of Change Conference held in London on 23 September, 1988 was opened by the Rt Hon Norman Fowler, MP, Secretary of State for Employment.

It was chaired by Brian Wolfson, Chairman of the National Economic Development Council's Tourism and Leisure Sector Group, Chairman of the National Training Task Force and Chairman of Wembley plc.

Speakers at the Conference were:

Allan Gilmour, Executive Vice President, International Automotive Operations, Ford Motor Company.

Scott Durward, Chief Executive, Alliance and Leicester Building Society.

Eric Hammond, General Secretary, Electrical, Electronic, Telecommunications and Plumbing Trade Union.

John Ashcroft, Chairman and Chief Executive, Coloroll Group.

Dick McBride, Ayr Small Systems Manager, Digital Equipment Scotland.

Ron Harris, Resources Director, Energy Business Systems Unit, Westinghouse Electrical Corporation.

David Stevenson, Managing Director, HRD International

The research which provided the basis for Part Two of this report and the case studies reproduced in Part Three were carried out by David Stevenson of HRD International and Alan Anderson, Associate Fellow of the Institute of Manpower Studies (IMS).
Dr Wendy Hirsh, a Fellow of the IMS, acted as an adviser.

The case studies were as follows:

Digital Equipment Scotland, Ayr
ICI Fibres, Doncaster
John Brown Automation, Coventry
Lep Group and Lep International, Epsom

Lucas Industries and operating units
Lucas Car Braking Systems, Pontypool
Lucas Car Braking Systems, Bouzonville, France
MB Group and Neath Industrial Components, Neath
Pratt & Whitney, Halifax, Canada
Reuters Holdings, London
Scottish Steel and Tube Works, British Steel, Glasgow
Westinghouse Electrical Corporation and AEG-Westinghouse Transportation Systems, Pittsburg, USA

In addition to the case study establishments, visits were made to:

Digital Equipment Corporation at Enfield, Connecticut, USA; Pratt & Whitney in Hartford, Connecticut, USA; and Westinghouse Productivity and Quality Center, Pittsburgh, Pennsylvania, USA

PART ONE

UNDERSTANDING THE NATURE OF CHANGE

Some would say that change can be stressful but that it leads to benefit in the longer run and should be welcomed. A strong message from the Conference was that change is inevitable. Competitive advantage is gained by those who see what needs to be done and change accordingly. Some established companies manage to change quickly: just as quickly as those which start afresh on a green field site. For others, history makes it difficult to evolve and emerge in a new guise and the companies have to face the trauma of major change or suffer decline.

It is widely accepted that the pace of change has speeded up in the 1960s, 70s and 80s. New markets and new producers have been accompanied by new products, materials and processes.

For some companies the process of radical change developed relatively unchecked over many years. For others, progress was interrupted during the early 1980s when their first concern was survival and they had to concentrate on lowering costs and, often, reducing capacity. After, it became clear that the cosy and, in some cases, not so cosy market niches they had established during earlier years were no longer viable. Neither were old management attitudes.

Coming out of the recession period, managers sought to adjust. The 'cold shower' may not have been welcome but it seems to have set a seal on the view of many managers that it is not possible to move back, to continue to muddle along or to seek change by just sharpening up here or reducing costs there. While in the past incremental change - transition - has been a sufficient basis for success, for the future something more all-embracing, something which is capable of achieving a transformation, may be necessary for many companies.

Many companies would recognise the need for change to be market driven. But radical action is taking new directions. The concept of the firm as a system for customer satisfaction is developing. This relates to the need for a thorough knowledge of the market and concern with total quality.

Applying this concept to organisational design leads to emphasis being placed on the interdependence of machines, people, departments and divisions. It leads to the development of a better understanding by people at all levels about the ways in which they affect customer satisfaction. It further leads to the development of people as a positive way of increasing competitiveness through a positive approach to change. The case studies are particularly interesting because they show how, in their search for success, some companies move progressively from 'hard' elements - technology, product development, price and quality to 'soft' elements including training, motivation, team working and organisational culture.

Part Two of this report provides a framework within which to consider what is needed to manage change. The case studies show how, starting in the early 1980s a number of companies have taken steps to transform their performance. The market should provide the impetus for change. But, paradoxically, for many companies, the currently more healthy economic climate can provide a major obstacle.

As Allan Gilmour of Ford, a conference speaker observed, "companies have a harder time doing what they want to do than what they have to do". It is important neither to allow inertia to dull the appetite for change, nor to allow custom and culture to prejudice a systematic appraisal of the changes required.

Change is a fact of life and does not care who it hurts
Allan Gilmour, Ford Motor Company

In the early 1980s we faced two alternatives, continued fine tuning ... or radical change and we opted for radical change
Ron Harris, Energy Business Systems, Westinghouse Electronic Corporation

Not everyone has to meet customers face to face. But would it not be a significant step forward if everyone acted as though they did?
Brian Wolfson, Chairman, Wembley plc

How can we configure our machines to service that market?
John Ashcroft, Chairman and Chief Executive, Coloroll Group

We are moving from the machine to the systems age. ... A lot of people go to work today and they don't know what the company's purpose is, or their purpose is. If you can identify that, you are able then to develop goals and objectives which the system can start to resolve
Dick McBride, Digital Equipment Scotland

Employers must realise that the notion of people at work at an undifferentiated mass with identical interests has gone for good ... Realising, releasing and developing those talents is the key to success
Norman Fowler, MP, Secretary of State for Employment

British industry has within it a wealth of uptapped talent
Eric Hammond, General Secretary, EETPU

Our staff have an appetite for change
Scott Durward, Chief Executive, Alliance and Leicester Building Society

PART TWO:

MAKING CHANGE HAPPEN

The individual steps taken by the case study companies and described by the Challenge of Change Conference speakers are brought together and listed below under seven headings: the key components of change.

Secure top level commitment to change

Diagnose change requirements

Promote the need for change

Plan the change programme

Enable change

Train for change

Maintain and reinforce the change programme

Managers will find it useful to compare the list and the more detailed action points which follow with the contents of their own change programmes. The action points are illustrated using examples from the case studies. The list does not represent a comprehensive change programme applicable in all circumstances. At any one time the complete package would be impossible to introduce. But it should help in the systematic planning of such a programme.

SECURING TOP LEVEL COMMITMENT TO CHANGE

In any substantial change programme the influence of chief executives as the driving force is clearly crucial. They must be involved in the definition of both targets and the changes necessary to achieve them.

Chief executives need to begin the process by creating a vision and by asking the fundamental question, "where are we now and where do we want to go?" Securing the commitment of the top team to the necessity for change and the path to be taken is a vital exercise that can only be undertaken by the chief executive.

ACTION: Create the vision

A vision is clearly required by companies which seek to make radical changes to achieve a transformation. It involves establishing new goals and setting the values by which they may be achieved.

Creating the vision takes time. Some case study companies held off-site "search" meetings, during which the vision was hammered out. Some found it desirable to state the vision in terms of a simple mission statement. For Westinghouse it was "to achieve world-wide leadership in our chosen fields by an emphasis on customer needs, technical excellence and manufacturing performance".

Some of the case study companies saw their old values as being reflected in problems with the reliability of their products, in their approach to quality, in their view that people were an expendable resource and in their views that communications were one way (downwards) and that management's function was to control. Their new values were orientated towards customers: quality was to be built-in; people were to be regarded as an asset; communications were to be open, two-way and candid; and management's role was to be one of enabling others.

The establishment of such new values required a complete overhaul of management practices, policies and procedures - a cultural realignment of the organisation.

ACTION: Spread the word

Commitment to a vision of change needs to be clearly stated and publicised, for instance through the circulation of a "mission" statement; it needs to be reinforced with articles in company magazines, staff circulars and in management speeches. In groups of companies, involvement from the centre is not always essential in this process, especially in decentralised groups with autonomous business units. It can be essential in centralised organisations, wherever change needs to be driven from the centre.

Top level commitment and detailed explanation and involvement within the unit concerned is absolutely vital. Without this, middle management, who are the engine room of change, will not support the change programme. At best, the change programme will be ineffectively communicated to other employees; at worst, nothing will be done.

ACTION: Provide continuity of commitment

Continuity of commitment needs to be made visible by the top management team. Simply delegating responsibility for change or producing mission statements will fail the continuity test and will be unlikely to generate real change.

Once the programme is under way, management needs to check progress against targets, to coach and encourage, and to look ahead to the next stage.

ACTION: Appoint a change agent

To move the process along more quickly in its early stages, it may be helpful to appoint a change agent. Essentially, change agents are used as catalysts for exploring issues, mainly through one-to-one discussion with key employees. Through the process of questions and answers, the change agent aims to create ownership and commitment to change and seeks solutions to problems. Total commitment to change can only be arrived at through involvement.

Among the case study companies the change agent has sometimes been an internal appointee, as in Scottish Steel and Tube Works, Digital or Lucas. However, there is a view that an internal change agent is exposed to some career risks and there are benefits of neutrality in using outside specialists, particularly when the aim is to explore cultural constraints.

Pratt & Whitney and Lep (and indeed Digital at its Enfield, USA, site) made use of outsiders. The external change agent can ask questions which insiders find it difficult to ask and is more likely to think the unthinkable.

DIAGNOSING THE CHANGE REQUIREMENTS

Diagnosing the change requirements has two purposes: the setting of objectives and the determination of the steps necessary to achieve those aims. It is an essential step and needs to be considered comprehensively if well thought out changes of one type are not to be undermined because essential, supporting changes are not put in hand. The actions to be considered look outward to the market place and competitors and inward to organisation and motivation.

ACTION: Understand competitors and competitive pressures

A key component of the diagnosis stage is an evaluation of where the company is against where it needs to be vis-a-vis its competitors. Lucas's Competitiveness Achievement Programme approach shows the value of competitor benchmarking.

Benchmarking exercises look at price, quality and delivery (for services as well as products). They look at what is known about competitors' productivity and cost structures. They look at strengths and identify weaknesses and set targets for achievement. They are dynamic in concept, taking account of the way in which environmental changes may affect the company in comparison with its competitors. Circumstances change and the experience of case study companies suggests that it is essential to allow for flexibility.

One of the key aims of the diagnostic phase is to establish what needs to be done to achieve benchmark objectives, as opposed to measuring the performance gap.

In the case of Pratt & Whitney's Halifax plant, two goals were adopted: to reduce conventional product cycle times by 80 per cent; and to reduce deviations from specification to one per cent of the level achieved by a conventionally managed plant. As is shown in the case study, considerable changes were necessary to meet these objectives.

Wider issues may include corporate goals, strategy and tactics. It may be necessary to consider, among other things, whether the company is best configured as a centralised or a decentralised concern. In the case of the MB Group decentralisation was associated with a process of management development - "empowering" local initiative.

ACTION: Establish the importance of quality

In every case study, quality was the subject of special attention. ICI Fibres at Doncaster has its own special quality programme, "Towards Manufacturing Excellence". Some, like Digital in Ayr, exemplified their quality performance by using their plant as a demonstration site.

Westinghouse had an internationally renowned Productivity and Quality Centre which contributed several billion dollars by way of corporate savings to improved performance. Although specific quality programmes are more usually to be found in manufacturing concerns, Reuters also had a quality programme, "Quality Comes First". Lucas Car Braking Systems, Pontypool aimed to be a "Total Quality Organisation".

ACTION: Consider the relationship between organisational structure and technology

All the case study companies have had to pay particular attention to their organisational structure and to their use of technology and have had to consider these in relation to their change objectives. Significant performance gains have been made through decentralisation, pushing responsibility down the line and cutting out layers in the organisational chain. Multi-skilled teams have often proved to be a more effective way of working.

In the case study companies, improving performance has had less to do with the application of sophisticated technology and more to do with organisational and methodological changes. The latter have often brought more immediate benefits. Lucas say that their productivity gains are 30 per cent attributable to technology and 70 per cent to manufacturing systems methodology. Most of the case study companies have been concerned not to become technologically dominated.

ACTION: Assess the contribution of better work flows

A commonly used way of improving performance has been work flow analysis.

In the case study companies this had taken a number of forms. Often, the introduction of such methods was closely associated with organisational and motivational aspects of a change programme, including team working, attitudinal changes, industrial relations changes and improvements to working practices.

Lucas Car Braking systems at Bouzonville had made imaginative use of activity analysis, so as to relocate functions around product families rather than around families of machines. Semi-autonomous manufacturing units were created with their own internal structure of 'Modules' and 'Units'.

Pratt & Whitney had used a similar approach in some of their mature plants - what they call "Flow-lining". MB Group at its Neath Industrial Components unit had done likewise, as did ICI Fibres.

ACTION: Look for opportunities to integrate using computer power

The computer-integration of companies is now extending from the workplace to customers and suppliers and, for some executives, back to their electronic offices at home. The ability to communicate using electronic data interchange up and down the supply chain is no longer an option in some industries.

ACTION: Consider the need to develop team working

The Lucas case studies refer to the effective use of Task Forces to analyse the need for and assist the process of change through the use of "semi-autonomous manufacturing cells, run by teams, Japanese style". These have helped replace the fragmentation, complexity and rigidity of existing organisation structures.

Pratt & Whitney is among the case study companies making use of team working. John Brown Automation restructured its operations to make use of project teams. Westinghouse extended the principle of team working to its financial staff, with considerable success. MB Group's Neath Industrial Components subsidiary runs courses in team working for its managers as part of its programme "to obtain greater managerial cohesiveness".

Other interesting developments in team working include Pratt & Whitney's computer-integrated plant at Halifax, which is run entirely by three teams of managerial, manufacturing and support staff in what they describe as a 'socio-technical system'. Digital at Ayr makes use of other advanced forms of team working, called High Performance Work Groups.

ACTION: Assess competence and training needs

Assessing performance may lead to the conclusion that managerial and shop floor skills need to be improved. The task goes beyond carrying out a simple skills audit. An evaluation of the skills required to carry out the proposed changes is also needed. Any new skill requirements which are identified will need to be met and the company may need to move quickly to recruit or train suitable staff.

ACTION: Analyse culture and attitudes to change

Attitudes to change are crucial, particularly those of the senior and middle manager, who must drive the change process. But the views of all employees need to be taken into account in evaluating a programme for change. Commitment to change is helped by consulting people. This is a sensitive process. Changing an organisation may require, among other things, the realignment of status, responsibilities and working habits. Some people seek to retain power by resisting change. The change programme has to recognise the possibility of such difficulties. In this the use of an outside change agent can be particularly helpful.

Other factors which may inhibit or prevent change include inappropriate reward systems, unsafe work, poor working conditions, boring and repetitive jobs, lack of opportunities for personal development, impersonal management attitudes and lack of feedback on performance and on achievements.

The importance of attitudinal change is thrown into sharp relief when competitive pressures lead companies to seek to move from being what can be characterised as a controlling to being a facilitating organisations. The controlling organisation is characterised by the way technology determines the flow of work and the division of labour and the inflexible way in which people work. The facilitating organisation, in contrast, is organisationally dynamic. Production systems are designed by technical and human resource specialists. The shape of the organisation is determined by the need for people to work positively together. Personnel responsibilities are carried by line managers and the organisation attaches high priority to developing people. Rewards are related to personal development and performance. The rewards of line managers are in turn related to the development of their subordinates. The contrast between controlling and facilitating organisations is illustrated by the scale of change some of the case study companies have made.

Some case study companies have had to settle for the long haul in their change programmes because they believe that they are unable to move faster along this road. Certain of the case study companies, notably Digital have been successful in introducing further change, precisely because they have already succeeded in creating a culture with a total acceptance of the essential need for change.

ACTION: Know what people are thinking

A number of the case study companies were convinced of the need to evaluate employee attitudes. This was sometimes carried out by using outside consultants, but was often the function of change agents. Feedback was obtained through special meetings and in some cases chief executives held regular meetings with randomly selected employees. These consultative arrangements were often augmented by the use of opinion surveys.

ACTION: Assess the potential for taking discretionary effort.

The concept of discretionary effort - that effort which an employee can give over and above the level necessary to fulfill contractual arrangements - is growing in importance as the need increases for organisations to make full use of all of their employees' capabilities. In Pratt & Whitney, tapping discretionary effort is one of the key goals behind its management training programme. Besides removing the petty regulations affecting employees - "the unnecessary don'ts in the rule book", a major effort has been made to allow employees greater self expression and encourage individual initiative.

PROMOTING THE NEED FOR CHANGE

Promoting the need for change requires a reinforcement of the vision and an explanation of the reasons for change and of the values, strategy and tactics which have been decided upon.

ACTION: Justify change

To justify the need for change the "why" of the change programme has to be understood. The reasons arise from diagnosis of the business case for change. The justification process should set out the need for change in a way that enables individual employees to relate their personal contribution to the overall programme.

When a company is doing well and has, perhaps, already come through a crisis of survival, as was the case with MB Group, further change can appear unnecessary. In such circumstances change can be unwelcome and strongly resisted if it is not adequately justified. As a general rule, change programmes appear to be more readily accepted when focused on opportunities and the need to secure a repositioning in the market place to ensure long term competitiveness.

ACTION: Explain to all employees

Next, how the change objectives are to be realised needs to be explained carefully to all employees. A poor explanation of the implementation of the programme can have a particularly adverse effect. Some of the case study companies were faced with industrial unrest as a result of inadequate explanation.

Change requires top level commitment, but eventually it has to be a collective effort. Total commitment to change can come only through common knowledge of what is required of people. People need to be made aware of the details of the change programme as early as possible. Some of the case study companies believed their change programmes would have been more effective if they had involved more people at an earlier stage.

ACTION: Work with internal customers

Almost all the case study companies have taken steps to get closer to their customers. However, some have extended the 'customer' concept to relationships within the plant, so that all working relationships are treated as 'customer' relationships. The Westinghouse financial staff formed 'Travel-In' groups to regularly visit their in-house 'customers', rather than waiting to be asked.

ACTION: Integrate supplier relations

Most of the case study companies had taken steps to get closer to their suppliers. In some instances this extended beyond issues of raising quality and improving deliveries to downloading production scheduling information, to enable the supplier to improve their service. In other cases, notably Pratt & Whitney, the companies trained their suppliers to make sure that the need to meet quality objectives was understood and to enable them to improve their efficiency through statistical process control.

ACTION: Work with external customers

The establishment of good customer relations has always been a key activity in every successful business. The case-study companies had taken this general principle further, in a deliberate attempt to consolidate relationships with their customers. It was being achieved in two basic ways.

The first involved the creation of project groups, as in Westinghouse and John Brown Automation, with designated responsibility for particular customers' projects. This enabled customers to monitor the progress of their contracts and to be provided with status reports from any member of the project team.

The second method was the creation of electronic links between the case-study companies and their customers, in much the same way as the companies had linked up with their own suppliers. The implications for competitors of this kind of relationship may be worth noting. In the future, gaining access to markets may come to have as much to do with the ability to provide electronic data interchange facilities as it has to do with products, prices, quality and delivery.

PLANNING THE CHANGE PROCESS

Change has to be carefully planned, with clear integration of all its elements. Partial change programmes, such as quality exercises, frequently run into problems and fade away because they are not part of a total system of change.

ACTION: Integrate all the elements

Transformation management demands the ability to integrate all the component corporate activities into a change programme. Although successful integration requires a supportive culture, there are many organisational changes which can help. The task starts at the top. The top management team needs to operate in harmony - an apparently obvious goal, but one which is difficult to achieve. Teamworking, matrix management and establishing firm internal customer/supplier relationships can provide a way ahead.

ACTION: Make better use of existing resources

Very few companies can enjoy the luxury of setting up on a greenfield site. The experience of the case study companies shows the importance of making better use of existing resources before committing new resources to the change programme. Most of them had some way to go in tapping the knowledge, experience and particularly the 'discretionary' effort of their employees, in rationalising plant layouts, equipment utilisation and in generally cutting out waste. A number of the case studies companies, notably Lep, Lucas and Westinghouse have shown what is possible.

ACTION: Identify opportunities for early success

Identifying areas of early success provides a major link between the planning stage and the execution of the change programme. Such successes are important in establishing programme credibility and in raising confidence. Early successes are more easily achieved by working through allies of change and by focusing resources and energies on specific issues.

Early successes demonstrate management's intention to push ahead and they also bring a sense of reality to the change exercise. Nothing succeeds like success.

Early successes at the personal level are important, too. Getting people to undertake tasks which stretch their abilities has been shown to be a useful method of bringing about a sense of achievement.

ACTION: Establish realistic time scales

In planning for change, timing is important. One important lesson of the case studies is that change takes longer than expected. This is due in part to the complexity of change programmes, but it has more to do with the capacity of individuals and groups to cope with and digest change.

Change involves a good deal of mental adjustment; for instance, in moving away from a confrontational industrial relations approach.

This has to be overcome in one way or another. The case study companies had various ways of dealing with the problem.

In some, change was considered to be less easily attacked and to be more manageable if broken down into small steps. "Progres par petits pas", as it was put at Lucas Car Braking Systems at Bouzonville. Or as another case study company, ICI, saw it, "you don't tell everybody what all the goals are on day one; give it to them in bite-sized pieces". Other case study companies, such as Westinghouse, went for a total change.

It is difficult to say which approach has the advantage in terms of the speed of change. Both approaches require careful planning.

ACTION: Provide resources for change

Good managers are always trying to strike a fine balance between resources used and resources needed. Under-resourcing can strike at the heart of the exercise. It is particularly easy to underestimate the time needed for planning and finding out what skill/knowledge is not available and will have to be bought-in.

Some case study companies have found it helpful to develop a central management resource to provide the necessary initial critical mass of competence to assist other parts of the company. Lucas Engineering and Systems Ltd provided a central manufacturing systems engineering skills resource along these lines.

At the outset it is relatively common to under-state the training requirements of a change process. This is in part inevitable, as the early stages of planning may not identify all the training needs. Similarly, the costs of recruitment and of making changes to, for instance, pay systems are more difficult to assess in the initial stages.

ENABLING CHANGE

Enabling change means creating conditions in which people willingly carry out changes so that the programme develops its own momentum. This is done through the following main enabling activities.

ACTION: Create open communications

An important step in generating support for the change programme is the creation of open communications. Open, two-way communications with clear and consistent messages provide the lifeblood of the successful change programme. Employees need to be told the truth. In one case study company, the marketing director complained that the company magazine referred to the loss of a particularly important contract. The personnel director's reply was "Our problem is, we have too much complacency around here. Everyone thinks we win everything".

ACTION: Create ownership of change

It is apparent from the case studies that employees often welcome change. But it is also sometimes the case that some managers do not initially welcome change. Management can be a weak link in the process of change.

Managing change requires managers to change and they can only do so successfully if they are aware of this necessity. The first step in ena-bling change is the establishment of trust among managers. This can be brought about through involvement in the creation of the vision and change objectives.

A number of the case study companies have found that generating ownership of change often requires decision-making to be pushed down the line. This may need to be reinforced. For example, expenditure authorisation levels may need to be adjusted, so that the decision-making process reflects corresponding levels of financial trust.

Creating ownership has become something of a catch phrase, but it is central to the process of changing attitudes, creating a sense of personal and team responsibility for actions taken. All of this is best secured through a process of involvement in which the individual's ideas are allowed to surface and be applied. Offering training and development, therefore, has a strong motivating effect, as well as building competence.

The process of empowering people and letting them have ownership of their ideas may be painful for some managers. Training, development, coaching and counselling are important if such changes are to be successfully carried through. This presents a considerable challenge to managers who have become accustomed to a hierarchical structure and who may say "now I'm told to coddle them".

TRAINING FOR CHANGE

Training is a major enabler of the process of change. If one of the goals is to create a flexible, responsive and adaptable organisation in which decisions are pushed down the line, those making the decisions must be trained accordingly. As one executive put it, "don't empower incompetence. Train, then empower".

The first step is to train and develop managers. While on occasion it may be necessary to send people on courses, as a general rule the case study companies aimed to train close to the job, using up-to-date, often purpose made, user-friendly, training materials.

In some cases high quality interactive videos have been produced in-house.

People who worked together were trained together.

ACTION: Train for leadership

Digital and MB Group, among other case study companies, have introduced specific initiatives to train managers for change. Pratt & Whitney's parent organisation, United Technologies Corporation (UTC), has involved 1500 of its managers from all over the world in a training programme focusing on leadership and attitudinal change needs. These programmes aim to develop the leadership characteristics which are considered fundamental to the successful management of change.

The UTC leadership course is built around the premise that markets are becoming increasingly segmented and competitive and that the need for flexibility of response requires an organisational approach which ensures that decisions can be made quickly. It is believed that this aim cannot be met without the involvement of people at all levels.

The UTC course takes managers through the creation of a vision, develops the notion of 'shared' vision and helps develop managers' willingness to use their initiative. It also shows managers how they can empower others and extend their influence by acting as facilitators and enablers. The training shows managers how to create and perpetuate a change culture.

Tough decisions are inevitable in the management of change, and training for leadership needs to provide for this. Change brings anxiety and uncertainty, which managers need to understand, particularly when the programme becomes exposed to criticism and obstruction. However unpalatable, the programme may involve redundancies and reassignments, and for this managers need to be mentally prepared.

ACTION: Develop line and personnel management skills

Increasingly, line management skills need to include the ability to develop people by identifying skill requirements, defining training needs, designing appropriate pay systems and introducing programmes to improve the selection of staff. Line managers in the case study companies had been trained to carry out day-to-day responsibilities which had previously been the province of the personnel or training manager. Consequential adjustments then needed to be made to the skills of personnel and training staff. Many needed to acquire an understanding of the ways in which people needed to be prepared for radical changes in skills and new career directions in companies which had undergone fundamental change.

ACTION: Train all employees

Vocational training for professional, technical and operational purposes (for instance, in the introduction of a new accounting system or the operation of a new machine) is an obvious need. Less obvious are the other needs of those who may be involved in the planning of the change process.

Companies such as Lucas thoroughly trained those involved in task forces or in multi-disciplinary teams on the redesign of processes.

Those companies looking for continuous improvement need people with skills in problem identification, determining priorities and problem solving. These people may also need considerable coaching in the early days, so that they can become more comfortable with their new responsibilities.

MAINTAINING AND REINFORCING THE CHANGE PROCESS

The process of change is not 'once and for all'. As markets and technologies change, regeneration of the transformation programme is essential. Incremental change of some operations will also be an important part of the overall programme, given the limitation of resources.

ACTION: Institutionalise the change process

Change needs to be made a way of life. The change programme must be institutionalised: implanted in the mission statement, in policies and procedures, and the subject of feedback on results through internal communications.

This process can be reinforced by the selection and, where appropriate, the advancement and promotion of appropriate personnel. If those expected to lead in the process of change are not committed or are incapable of managing change, then the process will disintegrate. Rewards need to be directed at those who change successfully.

ACTION: Train for continuous change

To ensure that management is preparing itself for tomorrow, companies need to carefully prepare succession plans and encourage those capable of supporting and stimulating further change. Managers and other employees need to be trained continuously, because competitors will not stand still and customer expectations will continue to rise.

In some of the case study companies, people were capable of exercising skills not associated with their immediate jobs, such as presentational skills. At Westinghouse and Pratt & Whitney, shop floor workers had access to VDUs to enable them to access training material and refresh their memories on the technical aspects of their jobs. At Digital, reorganisation of the plant demanded the enhancement of skills. After reorganisation there were few conventional job descriptions. At Digital, people are trained in advance, so that they change as their jobs develop.

The necessity for continuous training to ensure continuous change seems obvious. But the training budget is often the first to be cut when trading difficulties are encountered. Although this is understandable when survival itself is the consideration, training for change has to be seen as a vital investment. "We did our training for today five years ago" as one case study company put it. Halting the 'training for change' programme is to settle for the status quo and will eventually lead to loss of competitive position and failure.

ACTION: Continuously measure performance and review the change programme

The aim of the change programme must not be lost sight of: to raise competitive performance beyond that of the competition. This entails constant evaluation of the competition. Finally, the successful change programme ensures that achievements are measured, the programme is constantly reviewed and the process reiterated. A number of the case study companies believe it is only through this total approach to the management of change that they can be sure of a reasonable chance of beating the competition, which is showing itself to be tougher by the day.

PART THREE

A CASEBOOK OF CHANGE

Digital Equipment Scotland **17**

ICI Fibres **27**

John Brown Automation **37**

Lep Group and Lep International **44**

Lucas Industries **50**

Lucas Car Braking Systems, Pontypool **58**

Lucas Car Braking Systems, Bouzonville **67**

MB Group and Neath Industrial Components **77**

Pratt and Whitney **86**

Reuters Holdings **93**

Scottish Steel and Tube Works, British Steel **103**

Westinghouse Electric Corporation and
 AEG-Westinghouse Transportation Systems **114**

DIGITAL EQUIPMENT SCOTLAND

CREATING A HIGH PERFORMANCE WORK GROUP SYSTEM

This case study shows how one of the world's leading computer manufacturers with a 'high tech' organisation places the emphasis on people in its management of change. "Optimise the people, not the technology", is the motto at Ayr.

Digital shows how the use of high performance work groups can help manage the transition "from the machine to the systems age" for which they say, "we need to rewrite the text books".

Background

The American Digital Equipment Corporation (DEC) was established in 1957, and virtually created the minicomputer industry. Digital currently has six manufacturing sites in Europe. The only one in the UK, Digital Equipment Scotland, began production near Ayr in 1976.

The three major activities on the Ayr site are:

• Small Systems Manufacture (SSM) which makes a wide range of products, from personal computers to small general purpose computers;

• Field Manufacturing Information Centre (FMIC), which controls orders, customer and revenue management for DEC Europe;

• In-House Semiconductor and Test (VLSI), engaged in the plastic and ceramic packaging of silicon chips and the testing of chips.

Employment on the site has increased in almost every year, and in mid-1988 was close to 1,500. Further employment growth, of 10 to 15 per cent, is planned for 1989.

This case study concerns only the first activity, small systems manufacturing. SSM currently builds about 900 systems a week and ships them to customers in 18 European countries. The value of output doubled in 1987 and again in 1988. Over those two years, SSM's employment roughly doubled, to almost 500. It is planned to increase employment to nearly 600 in 1989 to support further significant increases in sales revenue and output volume.

One further relevant factor is SSM's current organisation structure, which breaks down into three product-based groupings. Each acts as an autonomous business unit, with its own manufacturing process and its own support functions, including business planning, master scheduling, personnel and finance. All three businesses also have support from a small SSM team, covering engineering and technology, quality, information systems, new products, finance, personnel, materials and programme management.

The need to manage change

Like all computer manufacturers, SSM operates in an environment of continuous but unpredictable change. Technological change in products and processes is the greatest single pressure. Product life-cycles are shortening rapidly. In 1989 alone, SSM expects to start up seven new products, maintain five existing products and "retire" three others. Over the next three years, SSM will also have to move towards micro-assembly technologies and higher-volume production. There is no option: "technology is integral to our survival".

SSM believes most companies, not only in high-tech sectors, will be in the same position in the 1990s. This case study is about how SSM goes about developing flexibility and capability to change. From SSM's history of technology-driven change it pinpoints times at which particular changes occurred which put the strategies to the test. Two such occasions are described. The first deals with a change in the product five years ago, which could have threatened the survival of the organisation. The second deals with a current product change, calling for Just in Time (JIT) manufacturing, to enable SSM's growth plans to be achieved.

The Context: SSM was originally set up in 1976 to carry out the final assembly and test of systems shipped from America and destined for DEC's European markets. Three years later (1979) it had become involved in the slightly more complex assembly, configuration and test of sub-assemblies. But in 1982 it was becoming clear that technology change would drastically reduce the volume of these operations. Ayr had the plant and the people (almost 300) but would soon have no product.

Positioning for success

By the end of the year SSM's management had persuaded the parent company of the need for a full manufacturing presence in the UK and of their own ability to be competitive with other DEC manufacturing plants worldwide. Digital agreed to begin manufacturing personal computers for the European market in Ayr, instead of exporting them from the USA. SSM set up a Project Group to decide how to prepare the organisation for the changes to come. These would be extremely wide ranging: different products; a shift from final assembly and test to manufacture; and associated new production processes. The group's initial idea was to "automate the hell out of it", making a very large capital investment.

At this point, the project group became aware of the experience of another Digital plant in Enfield in the USA, which adopted an approach to production based on high performance work groups (HPWGs). HPWGs are essentially the same as the well-known, but little used composite autonomous work groups advocated by the Tavistock Institute. As used in Digital in America, the HPWG is a multi skilled team of about twelve people, including among others engineers, operators and quality staff. The aim is to create work cells which are vertically integrated from assembly to test and to packing for delivery. In a HPWG, each operator is capable of building and testing the complete product "front to back". To quote SSM's Manufacturing Plan: "The process design emphasises product ownership by the individual operators, in the belief that the understanding and responsibility that this brings will maximise quality, enhance processes, highlight and resolve problems quicker, and provide a higher degree of job satisfaction".

In the event, the success of the American HPWGs and the risk of investing in potentially inflexible capital equipment to manufacture for an unknown and highly unpredictable product market, persuaded the Ayr project group to make their investment in human capital. They aimed to create "a highly-motivated, highly-flexible, highly-responsible workforce". As today's SSM managers argue: "people are flexible, robots are not. Involving people is the key to change, not technology".

The project group recognised that to move to HPWGs would not be a simple "quick fix". The concept was not only new to the factory, it was light years removed from what in the region is still blamed for so many failures to manage change, a "West of Scotland manufacturing culture", with traditional barriers between functions and levels of a hierarchy in which those at higher levels tell those at lower levels what to do.

HPWGs were thought to be a high risk investment. Managers and supervisors would be suspicious of a system which diminished their authority and responsibility. Operators might be fearful about accepting increased responsibility. Those who did accept the approach would need considerable retraining. It would raise questions about the robustness of the organisation's culture (of which more, later) and of its (then) functionally-based structure.

Introducing the change: Volunteers for the new HPWGs were sought and together began training in readiness for the new product. Then in October 1983 Digital announced that Ayr would not after all be given the personal computer manufacturing work. By this time, the plant's final assembly and test activity was beginning to run down, so it was again at risk. But within two months Ayr management had persuaded the company to let it take over production of the Micro PDP/11 from the Galway plant. A major "selling point" in Ayr's argument was the HPWG approach. Ayr had made the investment, and was ready to put it to work. The fact that HPWGs had been designed to produce a different product was seen as immaterial. SSM also believes that many who are sceptical of HPWGs' transferability to other sectors are mistaken.

The way the change was managed says a lot about SSM. The strategy was clear and coherent; SSM saw its long-term future in manufacturing for the European market. The effective organisation of human resources was integral to that market strategy, and HPWGs were to be the key means through which to achieve that effectiveness. Individual development was linked to team work and team work was linked to corporate objectives but SSM still had to prove that it could make the approach work. The training programme for HPWG members was extensive. Each operator received an average of eight weeks training, including induction and modules of "core tasks" training in all stages of manufacture from goods inwards to despatch of final product. Each module carried certification and trainees had to demonstrate competence in every module in order to become a certificated operator.

Difficulties were encountered. Some operators could not accept the transition from more traditional, (even though relatively flexible, by many standards) ways of working, and went back to their former work. Some managers found the process of consensus decision making time-consuming and frustrating. A few left the firm. SSM management also felt they made mistakes: the considerable investment in training should have been even greater; the communications process could have been improved for those still working on the 'old' products, to avoid some resentment of the new groups as a kind of elite. But a detailed, independent analysis of the introduction of HPWGs, conducted in 1986, concluded that, on balance, it had been a considerable success. First, it had achieved many of its intended objectives for the organisation, including:*

• a good quality product;

• production to schedule (which converted many sceptics);

• a satisfactory stockturn;

• a good reputation for customer service;

• rapid change in attitude and behaviour, at all levels;

• employees' understanding of their impact on the business;

• development of self-management at individual, group and intra-group levels;

• open communication within and between functions and levels;

• flexibility in skill development and in response to change.

Second, it also succeeded from the individual's point of view. As these criteria show, the intention was not one of conducting an interesting experiment in the application of socio-technical theories. It was to achieve real business targets while simultaneously offering the individual a development opportunity. As one operator put it*, the benefits were:

• the opportunity to do a variety of work in the group, other than manufacturing;

• the team coherence, which had not been known in the plant before;

• "employee ownership", which increased quality;

• close physical contact between functions;
• the multi-skilled nature of the work;

• the speed at which the working day passed as a result of the varied and rewarding tasks.

Managing continuing change and growth

When production started in 1984, SSM's organisation structure was functionally-based. This was seen to be inconsistent with the cross-functional, product-based, highly accountable but self-determining HPWG approach. The structure was therefore changed to one with a clear product focus, based on a series of small business units, each being accountable for achieving its own business objectives. Each had freedom to organise its work as it saw fit (not necessarily using HPWGs). The new organisation further encouraged the HPWG

These quotes are taken from an unpublished case study report, the basis of a forthcoming book, "High Performance Work Groups: The Digital Experience" by Dave Buchanan and Jim McGalman, Routledge.

approach of pushing decision-making and communications down to the lowest level possible.

The introduction of HPWGs made for a more flexible organisation, as well as more flexible work groups. But HPWG working arrangements appropriate to the products, volumes and production processes of 1986 were already becoming inappropriate in 1988, as fast-changing product technology was compressing size, reducing the number of parts, simplifying the manufacturing content, and raising the volumes to be produced over a shorter life-cycle. In place of hundreds of orders a week, SSM had to position itself to produce thousands.

These volume demands left no alternative to the adoption of a JIT-based approach to production, to permit reductions in work in progress and improved process control. SSM mounted pilot projects to find out how workflows needed to be changed to maximise the use of JIT without losing the intrinsic advantages of HPWGs. One pilot project involved five HPWG operators who were previously doing "front to back" build at their five individual work stations, producing two machines a day. The new product had to be produced at one an hour. As it was more difficult to organise JIT for five work stations than for one, a new HPWG layout was found to be necessary.

The five operators were asked to decide on the most effective layout. As a manager said "you get there quicker if you give the problem to the people affected". They were also told (again in typical SSM fashion) "you won't get it right first time; you may look silly at times, but keep experimenting". To help them get it right, they were taken to see JIT installations in other "excellent" firms, and given appropriate information and training (including ten half-days on a problem-solving course).

They came up with a layout which retains the "front to back" approach. Each operator carries out all five operations, moving from one station to the next. But they are now involved in a flowline process. Operators who have become used to working on their own now have to work as a team, with the attendant peer group pressures.

To enable them to cope with the change, operators have identified their own additional training needs: decision-making, team building and assertiveness. These will be provided, and the lessons transferred to the next step, when JIT moves from a pilot group of five people producing one product to 36 people producing five products. But SSM will not simply pass down the pilot group's layout to the new groups. It will expect them to make their own decisions, because "we don't want a standard way of doing things here. We want continuous improvement through constant change".

Early results point to success for the pilot group. But as one manager noted "it would be surprising if it wasn't a success, because JIT principles fit so closely with the Digital way of doing things. These include:

- decentralisation of functions;

- no end-of-line inspection;

- individual operator responsibility for quality;

- "front to back" production;

- certificated operators (judged on quality of output);

- decisions made closest to the workplace;

- ownership of the problem by people prepared to accept responsibility.

As was said. "JIT is about continuous change, people led. So is Digital". In other words, SSM is enabled to adjust quickly to techniques like JIT by the investment it continues to make in the flexibility and capability of its employees.

Developing the capability for change

These are just two instances of how SSM has managed key changes. While they are not "in depth" studies, they perhaps give a flavour of the Digital approach. Both have focused on the adoption and development of high performance work groups as a mechanism for change; not because HPWGs are necessarily the approach to adopt in all situations but because they exemplify two features of SSM's approach to change.

First, they illustrate the central importance which SSM attaches to the "people contribution" in managing change. Second, they indicate SSM's awareness of the importance, of structures which are flexible enough to respond rapidly to the challenges of the future.

What these examples do not do, as they stand, is to explain why HPWGs have been so successful in SSM, when similar mechanisms have failed elsewhere. Success can only be guaranteed if and when people are flexible enough to work in such structures, competent enough to cope with the new range of tasks inherent in them, and committed to making them work effectively. SSM's success has its roots in strategies designed to generate such attitudes, competences and commitment.

The next section outlines three aspects of SSM's approach to human resource development (HRD): developing an appropriate culture and management style; maintaining personnel policies and practices which support that culture and style and ensuring there exists within the organisation an HRD capacity to make things happen. However, there will be no discussion of specially-devised formal arrangements for communication, consultation and involvement. They barely exist because they are not necessary. To quote one HPWG member "those things happen naturally, by the way we organise our everyday work".

Developing a culture and management style

Unlike many companies, SSM has not had to face the difficult task of making fundamental changes to its corporate culture in order to manage change. Digital's founder gave the company a distinctive set of norms and values and a related style of management which have acted as a powerful and transferable "unwritten constitution" as the company has grown. These norms and values are consistent with the HPWG mechanism which was developed in the parent company. As they say at Enfield, in the USA, "we built the plant around the philosophy".

What SSM had to do was adopt and adapt the philosophy. Adaptation meant tailoring slightly the norms and values to local circumstances and, more recently, writing them down in a booklet for all employees (the booklet is reproduced as an annex to this case study). As the booklet notes, "Digital's philosophy and values have been, and will continue to be fundamental to our success". They are not merely for the converted, because "all employees share the responsibility for preserving Digital's values". Neither are they imposed. The booklet was produced on the basis of a day's discussion involving all employees.

To the outsider, some of the booklet's guidelines to employees and their managers are particularly evident in the way SSM does things. One is the emphasis on learning and the tolerance of mistakes which occur in the learning process. As one manager said, "this the easiest company in the world in which to gain forgiveness". Sharing information within the group and across the organisation is another; to quote again "our approach is to transfer our skills and understanding, not to protect them". Perhaps above all, valuing employees as people; the same manager said: "people are our assets, not commodities".

Putting these norms and values into writing was not a "flavour of the month" exercise. They remain a live matter of discussion. They have entered into the everyday vocabulary of employees at all levels. As one person observed "They are part of the language of change". They appear in the company's strategic plans, are made operational in structures like HPWGs and are seen - just as MRPII, JIT, TQC, etc are seen - as tools which can make a direct contribution to competitiveness. The values are embedded in the organisation's systems and practices. They underpin its success in managing change. They strongly influence its management style and they constitute a further link between individual and corporate goals.

Personnel policies and practices

SSM works hard at establishing and maintaining personnel policies and practices designed to produce and support the contribution and capability of all employees. Examples of this investment in human assets can be given from its policies on recruitment and progression, training and development, and rewards.

Recruitment and Progression: Organisations with strong corporate cultures,such as IBM and ICI, often produce recognisable "types". A consultant's report on Digital in 1981 identified the "Digital type" as "somebody who is innovative, somebody who is enthusiastic, somebody who is willing to work hard, someone who isn't hung up on structure, somebody who has absolutely no concern with educational background".

These criteria strongly influence selection procedures. For example, in selecting operators the first sifting of applicants is done by site personnel, using appropriate scientific methods. The final selection is likely to be by a mixed group of eight or ten employees (including operatives) in accordance with the maxim that this gives the selectors "ownership", and the successful entrant contact points.

The criteria used by these selectors reinforce the idea of a "Digital type":

• "we don't hire people who like static organisations" said a manager;

• "we're looking for attitudes and personality, not whether (s)he has six Higher Certificates"; said a manager;

• "could I work with this person? Would they fit in?" said an operator;

• "we look for potential; the biggest value of our approach is seeing someone develop" said a supervisor.

The key words which are found in the 'values' booklet are also used to determine progression within (but not up) the organisation. SSM works hard at performance appraisal. There is no single performance review pro forma; the different businesses develop their own. The criteria are fairly simple and predictable:

• quality of work done;

• quantity of work done;

• job knowledge (skills, flexibility);

• dependability;

• co-operation;

• initiative (readiness to solve problems);

• attitude (willingness to accept changes).

It is common throughout all the business units that reviews are carried out rigorously, possibly on a quarterly basis.

Training and Development. The commitment to training and development is strategic. Almost the first statement of intent in SSM's Long Range Plan is "to maximise the use of people, through the development of systems to transfer knowledge and skills". The adoption of the high performance work group approach makes a large training effort inevitable, because "we believe all the people should apply their brains to problems. And if you want people to make decisions, you have to be prepared to educate them". Last year about £1,000 a head was spent on direct off-job training (excluding salaries). This meant an average of eighteen days training per head; about 8 per cent of working time. One of next year's targets is that all managers should spend at least five days as a trainee and five more as a trainer.

Much of that effort is naturally focused on understanding the technology. An example would be the recent introduction of MRPII, in which SSM reached Class 'A' status in eighteen months. From the start, it took the view that "companies which do a superior job at educating their people about MRPII have the easiest time implementing its concepts so we should strive to educate 100 per cent of the people in the business about MRPII".

That is what happened, with managers and supervisors doing the training so as to ensure accountability and strengthen their own understanding. Forty people are now fully certificated and seventy-five partly certificated. Almost 200 sat the Spring examination of the American Production and Inventory Control Society. At least 30 warehouse staff have acquired at least one module; it gives them a recognised stepping-stone in their personal development.

But SSM also encourages people to learn and develop beyond their immediate and technical job needs. As a manager said: "When the future is unknown, you go for lateral growth in skills". So SSM will pay the course fees for education outside working time and offer a range of non-mandatory training for employees to take up if they choose. Employees are encouraged in many ways to develop the habit of learning, so as to progress within the organisation.

SSM is participating in a Digital Europe-wide initiative which has recently been introduced to develop the capabilities of a core group of thirty staff in the management of change. Candidates will spend a quarter of their time over a year on this development.

Rewards. SSM designs its reward system according to its guiding values and relates rewards directly to the contribution which people make. At the collective level, "single status" conditions apply not only in matters like canteen, sickness provisions and pensions, but also in the provision of cars: anybody can lease one. Overtime is worked but the commitment to "trust" is such that "it's your decision whether to do it or not, and if you do, to record it".

Pay is determined at the individual level and linked to the appraisal system. The process takes a lot of time, but the outcome is seen to be more relevant. SSM will pay for skills acquired and applied. It will not pay people to agree to accept change. It will pay for quality, but not for quantity of output.

Finally, supervisors and operators interviewed for the case study drew attention (quite unprompted) to a third dimension of reward, usually in comparison to their previous

employment, of working at SSM. The words they used were "excitement, informality, involvement .... and fun".

Human resourcing capability

This is the final piece of SSM's strategic jigsaw; the capability not only to identify how its human resource policies need to develop in order to satisfy corporate and individual needs but also to provide the expertise to make it happen. This strategic capability is critical, given SSM's view that change management is carried out by the whole workforce, not just by an elite group of managers.

Digital world-wide works to a ratio of one personnel staff member to eighty employees. This is seen as the input necessary to sustain people-based businesses undergoing continual change and development. The Ayr site (1500 people) has thirty-four staff in personnel, almost half of whom are professionals capable of managing an autonomous business. This is precisely what most of them are doing. SSM alone has five such staff serving the business units within it. Further, these personnel specialists are deeply involved in the organisation's planning processes at all levels. They are at the heart of the business. Digital world-wide places major emphasis on strategic planning, in order to position it to take advantage of discontinuities, and "people strategies" figure strongly in the process. SSM in fact produces three linked plans:

• Overview Plans: dealing with broad policy, up to 7 years ahead;

• Capability Plans: dealing with medium-term (3-7 year) issues;

• Operations Plans: covering what needs to be done in the short term (1-3 years).

All the plans are produced by cross-functional forum groups. Each group has a personnel specialist member. Every plan emphasises the "people" issues, in a bid to support business success by "maximising the use of people through the development of systems to transfer knowledge and skills" (as SSM's Overview Plan puts it).

Another extract from the Overview Plan also explains much about SSM. To the question "how would we employ our organising principles to make SSM and our function more competitive?", it responds:

• continue the development of (High Performance) Work Systems;

• continue moves towards skill-based pay;

• implement a continuous training programme;

• review and share our values, beliefs and philosophies;

• implement information systems and management systems to support the above.

In total, this emphasis on norms and values, training and development and support capability adds up to a major continuing investment in positioning the business to manage change through people. It is an investment strategy based on the precept that the unexpected will always happen but that when it does the organisation will already have in place the flexibility, competence and commitment to cope with it.

HANDBOOK GIVEN TO ALL EMPLOYEES
OF DIGITAL EQUIPMENT SCOTLAND:
"DIGITAL'S PHILOSOPHY AND VALUES"

INTRODUCTION

From the start, shared values have been important to Digital. Digital's philosophy and values
have been and will continue to be fundamental
to our success. This booklet has been prepared
to help us clarify and share our philosophy and
values. We believe in the ideals stated here and
recognise that sometimes they're not achieved.
Through discussion, we can identify differences
between "what we say" and "what we do" and
start to change. All of us share the
responsibility for preserving Digital's values.

People

People are as important as business success.
Digital cares about employees and their
families' well-being.

Respecting customers, providing useful
products for society, being a good neighbour
and protecting natural resources are examples
of Digital's caring about people outside the
company.

Therefore, all employees are expected to treat
people justly; respect the rights of others;
respect people's differences; be responsible
citizens. In addition, managers/supervisors are
expected to ensure the safety of employees,
customers and the general community; take
affirmative action in providing equal
opportunity for promotion and employment for
all persons regardless of race, colour, creed, sex
or age; value employees as people not simply as
employees; take action to ensure that the
corporation is a good citizen of the host
community and nation.

Honesty

Trust is the basis of quality relationships among
employees and between the company and
stake-holders, customers, OEMs, suppliers,
vendors, governments and host communities.

Honesty is the principal means of establishing a
climate of trust.

Therefore, all employees and managers/
supervisors are expected to be honest not only
technically but also in the implications and
impressions left with people inside or outside
the corporation; make only the commitments
they can keep; be candid, open and truthful.

Profit

Profit provides the money we need to survive,
grow and develop. With profit comes the
opportunity to hire good people, produce
useful products, and give shareholders a just
return on their investment.

Therefore, all employees are expected to understand how their work contributes to the corporation's profitability; be as productive in their
work as possible. In addition, managers/
supervisors are expected to ensure their
groups' contribution to the corporation's
profitability; make decisions that balance "long"
versus "short term" business results.

Quality

Quality is our competitive edge. We value the
excellent performance of our people and our
products.

Therefore, all employees are expected to produce quality results; value quality performance
more than credentials, seniority, or status
symbols. In addition, managers/supervisors
are expected to hire the best qualified people
and develop them further; demand and reward
excellence.

Communication and simplicity

Our success depends upon our ability to be
responsive and flexible in a rapidly changing
environment. Open communication, simplicity
and clarity are essential.

Therefore employees are expected to
communicate all significant information to the
appropriate people; be direct; have clear work
goals and measure against them regularly. In
addition, managers/supervisors are expected to

use the simplest organisational structures and processes necessary to get the work done; be accessible; listen to and help employees with work related problems and concerns; share information within the group and across organisation lines; give usable feedback, both positive and negative; avoid overlap in work goals; work with employees to set clear goals and measure against them regularly.

Responsibility

People perform best when they "own" their own work. Digital values individual freedom and responsibility.

Therefore, all employees are expected to take responsibility for their own work; establish clear work goals with their managers; take initiative; stand up for what they are convinced is right. In addition, managers/supervisors are expected to delegate authority; provide opportunities for individual and team contributions; encourage and reward initiative; measure employees' performance against goals; hold employees accountable for proposals, once accepted.

Learning

There is always more to learn and do. Continuous development and learning are valued.

Therefore, all employees are expected to realise there is always room for improvement, never room for complacency; seek opportunities for development. In addition, managers/supervisors are expected to provide challenges for employees; foster development by providing opportunities for learning; tolerate mistakes which occur as part of learning.

Competition and conflict

The best ideas succeed. The comparison and clash of ideas is valued as a means of obtaining the best results.

Therefore, all employees are expected to accept conflict as normal; use conflict for positive results; incur the risk that comes with presenting new and different ideas. In addition, managers/supervisors are expected to encourage innovation; make conflict productive.

Co-operation

No one can know or do everything. Team play and co-operation provide the necessary synergy for success and the balance for internal competition.

Therefore, all employees are expected to ask for and offer help and support; be team players; accept modification of ideas; act in the best interest of Digital as opposed to protecting "turf". In addition, managers/supervisors are expected to create the climate for team play and collaboration.

ICI FIBRES

IMPLEMENTING A CHANGE STRATEGY

This is a case study of change in a highly-unionised, capital intensive, continuous process plant in Doncaster. By 1981 the plant was clearly uncompetitive, having never performed at maximum output in 25 years. The study explains how the plant has transformed its performance. This required astute leadership, commitment and pragmatism. The approach has been based on a clear vision of what needed to be done and then taking it 'step by step'.

Background

ICI's has been one of the world's most notable 'management of corporate change' success stories of the past decade. This case study is about one small part of that organisation, the man-made fibres manufacturing plant in Doncaster, (hereafter referred to for convenience as Doncaster). The important point to bear in mind throughout is that, while Doncaster's recent success in managing change has been to some extent influenced by changes in the wider organisation, it has essentially been of its own making.

Doncaster was opened in 1955 for the continuous process production of nylon fibre, so it is now a comparatively elderly plant. It was part of ICI Fibres Division, which in ICI's major reorganisation of January 1987 became one of the businesses within the Chemicals and Polymers Group. Doncaster is now one of four manufacturing sites within the Fibres Business. There are two other plants in the UK, and one in Germany. Including its HQ at Harrogate, the business employs 7,500 people.

Doncaster takes its raw material, nylon 6:6 polymer, from the group's Wilton site and heats, melts and extrudes it to produce in the region of 1,000 tonnes of nylon fibre a week. Nylon fibre is sold for use in the manufacture of carpets, clothing and a variety of high performance technical products. Competition in these markets is intense, and is affected by the long-standing existence of spare production capacity world-wide.

The structure of the organisation is of some relevance to the changes at Doncaster. For many years Doncaster functioned simply as a production unit, making what was required of it. Over the past four years it has become much more closely integrated with the businesses which it serves and has become heavily involved with customers.

In 1988 employment was about 1250, of whom around 75 per cent were process operators. The plant, which has always been 100 per cent unionised, is situated in a region which has experienced heavy job losses and major disputes in all its traditional industries: coal, steel, railways and engineering.

Pressures for change

The case study is about the management of gradual change within the organisation, in the context of a relatively constant but always hostile external environment. The region's industrial relations climate was a significant factor. It covers the period since 1981 when the current works manager became one of two managers appointed with the clear remit to "sort it out, or close it down".

Excess production capacity has been a feature of the nylon industry world-wide for many years, despite repeated rationalisation and major reductions in employment. Competition to meet customers' demands for low-priced, high-quality fibre has therefore been fierce. Technology has hardly changed the basic production process in several decades. After the mid-1970s, the oil-dependent industry became unprofitable as a consequence of a succession of oil price increases.

In 1980, ICI Fibres lost £86m, and this raised a fresh question-mark against Doncaster's existence. The plant had contributed significantly to the loss, both by its chronically poor yields - it had never reached anything approaching capacity output in its 25 years - and by its increasingly poor industrial relations record. A serious strike in 1979 caused many ICI managers to regard the plant as unmanageable. That record was fuelled both externally, by the regional industrial relations climate, and internally, by repeated threats of closure. As one manager recalled, "at that time, the plant had a death wish about it". However, the division decided to try another change of its top management.

The two new appointees were both line managers with experience of introducing change elsewhere in ICI. They had been heavily involved in implementing ICI's Manpower Utilisation and Payment Structure (MUPS) at a trial site in 1967. After initial familiarisation with the plant, their first decision was to develop a "Strategy For Change", aimed at "focusing not on where we were then, but where we wanted to get to".

Determining a strategy

"Where they were then" was in a plant with increasing and uncompetitive unit costs. Where they wanted to get to, over 5 years, was first a surviving, then a profitable, then a first-class Doncaster plant. Their strategy for getting there would have six main elements:

- operations improvements;

- better manning levels;

- more appropriate organisation;

- improved management control;

- getting closer to the customer;

- redefinition of standards and expectations.

Each element was to be tackled simultaneously; indeed, the final one was generic to the others. For each area, specific improvement targets were set, with appropriate time scales. The key objectives were then shared with senior managers, but the whole strategy initially was not made known within the plant. Instead, its introduction was made to appear as a series of discrete, achievable initiatives; "otherwise, there is a danger of overloading line managers". But, once the task had been broken-down into achievable elements, it was considered vital to make them known to all those involved: "tell people what you intend to do. You have to challenge their expectations and norms if you hope to change them".

Implementing the strategy. The first five years : challenging expectations

The new works and operations manager set guidelines for managing implementation. In the early stages, about the first two years, the operations manager would be seen to be personally directing the changes. This was "to demonstrate that change was necessary and led from the front" and, in view of the poor state of management morale in the plant, to give firm, top-down decisions, to "show people you do mean business, but constructively".

The expectation was that, once this approach had achieved some successes, leadership could be widened to include others, not least because "as an individual, you can only do so much", and because the overall approach would need to be made more participative. For example, "we did consider setting up joint working parties. In the right circumstances they are an excellent device; they can short-circuit so many things. But it was too soon to expect jointness to work in 1982".

Assuming this second, participative stage was making progress, that would be the time to encourage people more generally to "own" the initiative and take over some responsibility for driving it forward. At that point, a lot of training would be necessary. But not until then, because "in the early stages, in a situation as hostile as that, training is almost an irrelevance. But its significance alters over time. In the current stage (1988), training is supremely important".

In retrospect, these self-imposed guidelines were largely adhered to, though not in the clear-cut way they are presented here. The "top-down" approach had to go on for some considerable time, in part due to a chronically difficult industrial relations climate. Joint Working Parties were attempted too soon, and failed. Training might beneficially have been stepped-up earlier than it was.

But the concept of a strategy, with measurable targets and a pragmatic approach to management style, allied to a strong sense of timing, remained valid and proved successful. Progress towards some of the specific targets set under each main element of the strategy can be outlined.

Operations improvement. Even when it had a strong order book, Doncaster had never achieved output levels remotely approaching its capacity. The first essential was to get men and machines working together more effectively. So evident was the potential for improved yields, and so important was it to change expectations that the works manager felt he could confidently set improvement targets first, then analyse the true possibilities later: "keep it simple, and achievable. You can always refine the target later".

Two examples of this approach may be given. The first concerns the failure rate of the melter units which processed and extruded the raw material (nylon polymer). The plant had over 300 such units. They were expensive to buy, and when they failed their change over time was about 16 hours. In 1981 the average melter life at Doncaster was under 2 weeks; 30 per cent were failing on their first day.

The operations manager's view was that this situation had little to do with the quality of the units, but was mainly caused by sloppy operating practices. He therefore set a target: to halve the weekly failure rate. This "unrealistic" target was regarded with disbelief but within a year was achieved. The many possible reasons for failure were painstakingly analysed and acted upon. In 1988, the first day failure rate was around 10 per cent and the average life had reached 10 weeks, without significant investment or training costs.

A second example concerned another critical part of the process, the draw-wind machinery which stretched the yarn fine and wound it onto spools. In 1981 the average weekly output was less than 8 tonnes per machine against a theoretical maximum of 20 tonnes. The operations manager again suspected that working practices were inefficient, set an initial target of 14 tonnes, then set up, selected and chaired a working party to analyse the problem. "Nobody had recognised or thought about the theoretical maximum output. Their norms were changed". So was the target, to 16 tonnes. Output in 1988 had reached that level, though progress had been more gradual than that which had been achieved in the melter units.

Manning levels. In 1981 the works and operations managers, based on their experience elsewhere, knew that the plant was overmanned as well as under-utilised. Total employment was 1350. Manning standards were not properly related to work content. This time, however, the approach was to analyse and measure the situation in advance of change, because "not to know what the efficient level of manning is, is a disaster". An extensive programme of work measurement was introduced. As a result, in 1983 with output increased by 12 per cent but without any redesign of jobs, the revised manning standards were such that 200 employees took voluntary early retirement.

Organisational change. Doncaster management took the view that inefficiencies such as those outlined above were a result of deficiencies in the competence of managers or in the way they were organised, or both. In 1981 it looked like both, and in the works manager's words "to all intents and purposes management didn't properly exist here". The works manager quickly reduced the number of top management jobs from six to four. The personnel and administration functions were combined, and the engineering function was divided between development engineering, which subsequently report to the technical function head, and maintenance engineering, which report to production. The top management group then formed a think-tank to review the work of the next layer of 44 managers and professionals. After 18 months, the content of the jobs of 42 of these had been changed to a greater or lesser degree.

Management control. Change could only be maximised if the re-shuffled management team actually managed. By 1981, despite the considerable efforts of the previous works manager, line management had virtually lost control on industrial relations issues. They were simply being bypassed, or were passing on the responsibility to personnel or to the works manager. At the lower level, first-line supervisors were not seen by anybody as being part of the management team.

At that time operators were represented by nearly 50 shop stewards, who tended to communicate to top management through personnel, or directly, but not through the line. The operations manager decided that their proper route should be through line management, beginning at supervisor level. To make that happen, he introduced a "closed door" policy both for himself and for the personnel function, (which was also given lesser prominence by the restructuring of the top team). Over the next 5 years the number of stewards was almost halved. As a result of these changes "managers stopped passing the buck and began to grow". While the plant's industrial climate was not reformed overnight, at least there were no major stoppages from then on, a marked contrast to what was happening in other local industries.

In the nylon fibres industry the first line supervisor's position is especially important. They are traditionally drawn from the ranks of operators, many of whom are highly-skilled. In 1981, Doncaster's team of supervisors did not measure up to the task ahead. They could hardly be otherwise. They were not trained for their new role. Their role was in any case not clearly defined. They were not regarded as part of the management team, either by middle management or by the shop floor. Their span of control (25 process operators per supervisor) was excessive; and their job description did not require them to move outside the one area or "cell" to which they were appointed. (There were another 12 cells in the total process).

The operations manager sat down with the middle managers to write their supervisors' remits. The supervisors, too, were closely involved in the process. The new remits established supervisors firmly within the management team. The concept of a Doncaster process supervisor (as opposed to a cell supervisor) was established, to break down artificial barriers and create greater interchangeability between cells, to encourage understanding of the needs of other work areas and to enhance the co-ordination of the supervisory team . To support this redefinition, a major training programme was introduced, the content of which placed special emphasis on interactive skills.

Here again, achievement of change was often a slow, grinding process. By 1986, the number of process operators per supervisor had been reduced from 25 to 16 (it was subsequently reduced to 14). By no means all of the 64 supervisors were of managerial calibre; they had been selected against other criteria. For some, the duality, whether they were operators or managers persisted, not least because it persisted within management and on the shop floor. As the works manager reflects, "that is the most difficult part of the culture to change".

Getting closer to the customer. Through customer technical liaison (CuTech for short) great strides have been made in improved customer relations. The philosophy adopted was to put the effort into understanding the customers' needs, in terms of both product and service, and then to satisfy them. This positive approach replaced the reactive one of responding to complaints. Customers were actively encouraged to visit the plant: "it's good for our employees to see the real people who pay their wages". Employee exchange visits were arranged. Customers buying high performance technical products increasingly conduct rigorous quality audits: "the whole works knows it is on trial every time".

Standards and expectations. No special initiatives were introduced under this fifth aspect of the strategy. The strategy's whole purpose was to change standards and expectations and this intention was integral to every initiative taken. In 1981, many of the problems at Doncaster were a consequence of wrong attitudes at all levels. To begin to change those attitudes for the better, it was first necessary to get rid of some ingrained expectations. The strategy identified three kinds of approach which needed to be changed:

from:

- find reasons for inaction and failure;

- accept comfortable norms;

- nostaglia.

to:

• identify problems to be overcome to achieve success;

• set challenging goals;

• look forward.

By 1986, although a great deal remained to be done, expectations had been gradually but fundamentally changed by these initiatives. Managers recognised that a new, no-nonsense but participative style of management had become established. Doncaster had succeeded not only in surviving, but taking advantage of a market upturn to return to profit in 1984. In terms of the divisional remit of 1981, the plant had been "sorted out".

Implementation: the second five years, "Delivering the Promise"

The strategy after about 1986 had two main strands. The first was to continue to pursue all the main themes of the original strategy and to generate continuing improvements in operating performance. (In fact, output doubled from 1980 to 1988, while unit production costs, in real terms, fell slightly over the period.) The second was to build on these successes and develop a strand of the strategy with a more confident, outward-looking approach and a growing emphasis on the standards and expectations of customers, as well as employees.

In the first five years from 1981, Doncaster had to make its own luck. In the first half of the second term, it was able to take advantage of a rather more favourable operating environment. While some external factors, including world over capacity, technology, and competition remained constants, others differed from 1981. Market demand was generally more buoyant. The fibres business had developed excellent new yarns for the carpets and technical products businesses. Changes in ICI's organisation structure gave Doncaster a more commercial role. The regional industrial relations climate, from which no firm could totally isolate itself, became markedly less hostile.

Internally, Doncaster's approach to managing change looked very different from the strongly "top-down" early years. With a more effective management structure, with the use of group working, and with changed expectations the original approach was less necessary.

The change is apparent in the quality initiative, "Towards Manufacturing Excellence", which was introduced during this period. The main themes of the initiative are reproduced in Figure 1. It echoed all six themes of the original strategy. The goal was not just to change expectations but to raise them. The new language of change talked about "unlocking everybody's potential". There was a "mission statement" (Figure 2); this would have been ridiculed five years before. Slowly, the culture was changing.

The remainder of the case study looks at some of the policy initiatives being introduced to "unlock potential". Being part of a larger organisation can be of benefit but it can also impose some limitations on the range of policies which can be deployed. For example, divisional headcount limitations and company-wide pay structures may not permit variations which seem appropriate at individual plant level. So, Doncaster is moving fast in other areas, such as work organisation, employee involvement, communications and training; a very different agenda from 1981.

Work reorganisation. One example of work reorganisation shows how far Doncaster has gone "Towards Manufacturing Excellence" (TME). The production process is literally a vertical sequence, beginning with the input of raw material to hoppers situated on the top floor of the plant. When melted, the material moves down a floor for extrusion, then moves vertically down another floor for spinning. The manning of each successive stage is distinct, with no real contact between the operators working at different stages in the production process.

The aim is to introduce a vertical organisation, with some operators linking between extrusion and spinning. This would satisfy all three of TME's objectives. By strengthening the "internal customer" concept, it would give

ICI FIGURE 1

TOWARDS

MANUFACTURING EXCELLENCE

QUALITY	LOW COST	MANAGEABLE FLEXIBILITY
- HIGH PERFORMANCE PRODUCTS	- RIGHT FIRST TIME	- REMOVAL OF ROADBLOCKS
- PRODUCED SAFELY AND CONSISTENTLY TO SPECIFICATION	- ZERO BREAKS	- MANAGEMENT CONTROL
- CUSTOMER SERVICE SECOND TO NONE	- MINIMUM EFFECTIVE MANNING	- ALIGNMENT OF INDIVIDUALS NEEDS WITH WORKS AND BUSINESS REQUIREMENTS
	- FOCUSED ORGANISATION	

greater recognition of quality. It would achieve lower cost by reducing the minimum effective manning levels. It would result in greater manageable flexibility by removing roadblocks and increasing management control.

This initiative also illustrates significant differences in the change management processes, compared with 1981. A working party has examined the possibilities, and those concerned have been involved in the debate. The preference is that operators themselves should help to decide how to reorganise their work vertically. There would be a major training requirement, for which a capability now exists in the plant (see below).

Employee Involvement. In the beginning, involvement policies would have been useless and could have been damaging. Throughout the whole period, however, the Works Manager's clear long-term aim has been to say to people, "I want you on board" to make people feel part of a club, to give them opportunities". But the timing had to be right, with sufficient people wanting to be on board. The time is now thought to be right for this approach. Joint working parties have now become a prominent feature of the way Doncaster tackles problems. After a string of failures, the significant breakthrough came with an 'Achieving Higher Standards' working party in 1985. This succeeded because it was timely; by then expectations had been sufficiently changed and it was focused: both its members and its remit were carefully selected.

It was also supported. Instead of being led by the works manager, an independent consultant was deliberately brought in to 'free things up',thereby defusing the potential for friction and the associated loss of momentum. As the works manager put it, "an analogy is using a Driving School to teach members of the family to drive". Participants in these cross-functional groups were encouraged to use their learning to start up sub-groups in their own work areas. The joint approach was also adopted to secure more specific change aims, such as BS 5750 (successfully achieved) and Zero Defects (significant progress has been made, one customer has awarded the plant its own plaque for quality products).

Operators have become increasingly involved. For example, operators are now active in the BS 5750 initiative, which was originally perceived as an issue for technicians. Another example of people wanting to "join the club" was provided when an open invitation was made to all employees to tour the Wilton site (which produces most of Doncaster's raw material) as its "customers". The number of volunteers exceeded all expectations, and both customers and suppliers benefited by better understanding each others' practices and problems. Similarly Doncaster's own customers are increasingly welcome at the plant, where they are likely to be shown round by one of the new process training instructors, (see below).

The beginnings of a 'snowball' effect have become evident. The more the offers of involvement, the greater the acceptance. The greater the involvement, the more apparent the effect on attitudes. The more attitudes change, the greater the unlocking of (often unsuspected) potential. As one manager put it "we have in the past underestimated the intelligence of the shop floor". But it is not only shop floor talent which has been released; the manager concerned was one of several whose own potential was unlocked by the participative approach.

Communications. From 1983 onwards a lot of effort was put into informing individual employees about business prospects, order books and profitability. A "cascade" briefing system was introduced but it had variable success. At that time, the messages were sometimes unpalatable, most of the audience were not yet ready to listen and, despite the training they were given, most supervisors did not see communications as their job.

The situation has improved, albeit slowly. Some managers work harder than others at communications. As one enthusiastic manager put it, "we must use every means to involve everybody in managing change". So Doncaster is taking steps to improve its communications.

Training for excellence. Communications can be seen as a form of training. Traditionally, Doncaster's commitment to training left something to be desired. Indeed training, or the

1   In selling to a customer we accept responsibility for fully understanding his needs in terms of both product and service, and for satisfying those needs as agreed.

2   We will achieve this safely and in the most cost-effective way.

3   We acknowledge our obligation to ensure that every employee of ICI Fibres understands and shares in personal ownership of these commitments.

perceived lack of it, had given rise to some industrial relations friction and had at times been more successful in hardening attitudes than in changing them.

Three recent initiatives linked to the "Towards Manufacturing Excellence" programmes (see Figure 2, above) have been designed to change this situation. The first is the appointment of a senior line manager as full-time training and education manager. His brief covers the development of training, the improvement of communications, and the co-ordination of quality initiatives, all of which are seen as interlinked means" ... to unlock potential and change attitudes". This appointment is widely regarded as a major statement of management's intention to seek participative change.

The second, related initiative is the appointment in late 1987 of 16 former operators, to be full-time Process Training Instructors (PTIs). They replace a system in which operator training was largely carried out on a part-time basis.

The 16 PTIs, four per shift, were selected from 120 applicants. After two weeks' instruction in training techniques they were first sent out into the plant to train each other on all operations, to enable them to be effective anywhere in the plant. They then jointly developed training modules to ensure a common approach to the training of all operators. Their remit covered training in safety, quality and the use of fork lift trucks as well as the full range of operator training.

It is not anticipated that there will be a shortage of demand for training from new recruits or as a result of the introduction of new machinery and manning arrangements (for example, the new vertical manning organisation referred to above has its own training needs). However, very much in line with the views of the new training manager, the PTIs see their role as being wider than instruction. To quote them:

• on quality, "we will take the blinkers off people and show them the effect they have on other people's jobs";

• on training, "not just telling people what to do, but telling them why they are doing it";

• on communications, "that's a major part of our job. This plant has come a long way from a 'you will do' style of management. We have to make sure people's attitudes keep on changing".

The third training initiative concerns the all important supervisors, some of whom still have to come to terms with their management role, (which will itself be affected by the appointment of the new PTIs). The aim is to encourage their continual self-development. This involves a mix of formal training (including team leadership and time management), more active involvement in cascade briefing (and further training in appropriate techniques), overt delegation of management responsibility (for matters such as safety meetings) and opportunities to act in working groups to reorganise work (for instance the "vertical working" referred to in the section on "work reorganisation", above).

An interim assessment of change

By any measure, this has been a successful "management of change" story. Standard performance measures show (see Figure 1) consistently increasing output and productivity, and stable real unit costs. Indicators of product quality are improving. Last year, in highly-competitive markets, Doncaster achieved a 7 per cent margin on turnover.

Conventional manpower indicators of performance also show progress. While labour relations remains a thorny issue, the serious disputes which threatened to close Doncaster in 1981 are no longer a feature of the plant. Labour wastage rates, absence levels and accident rates are down.

Less quantifiably, attitudes are slowly changing. The plant no longer has a "death wish". Management are much more confident in their task. Employees recognise and welcome the increasingly participative management style.

In terms of managing change, a number of key themes emerge from, and have contributed to, this success. These may be summarised as:

• decide where you need to get to, and develop a strategy for getting there;

• make it crystal clear to everybody that change is necessary, and why it is necessary;

• tell people early on what you intend to do, to achieve change;

• set firm targets in areas where early success is achievable;

• keep the changes simple; "don't be too smart with the options";

• take it slowly; "it takes a long time to get change";

• lead from the top, but don't think you can do it all - so make use of consultants, where appropriate;

• free up management structures to help change along;

• fit the management style to the situation;

• changing attitudes is management's task.

JOHN BROWN AUTOMATION

FROM CONVENTIONAL MANUFACTURER TO DESIGNER OF AUTOMATED ASSEMBLY SYSTEMS

JBA started as a conventional machine tool company and is now a designer and builder of automated assembly equipment and systems.

The case study shows how JBA grew out of an established traditional engineering culture. The case study describes the new organisation adopted by the company and its dependence on recruitment of graduate level engineering specialists. Communications have been improved and an enhanced training effort has helped to sustain the 'momentum' of the three fold increase in output which the new company has enjoyed since its foundation in 1985.

Background

John Brown Automation, based in Coventry, UK, is one of the UK's leading designers and builders of automated assembly equipment and systems.

John Brown Automation has a turnover of £12.5m (1988), 60 per cent of which is accounted for by exports. The company employs 130 people, some two thirds of whom are qualified engineers at either HND or graduate level. In 1988, although still a relatively young company, JBA received the Queen's Award for Technological Achievement.

The company was founded in 1983. Until that time JBA existed as an integral part of Wickman Engineering Ltd, a subsidiary of the John Brown Engineering Group. In the early 1980s the Group was faced with a number of financial and other difficulties brought on by the recession and underwent a process of rationalisation prior to its takeover by the Trafalgar House Group in 1986. One result of this rationalisation process was that the Group's machine tool interests, a key part of Wickman Engineering, were largely sold off. Some sixty employees of the machine tool operation were retained to form John Brown Automation.

Introducing change

The case study shows how the company has become a successful project-based service organisation in the automation business, having previously been a product-based manufacturing concern making machine tools and related components.

Prior to the formation of JBA the parent Group devoted a great deal of attention to rationalising Wickman Engineering, which reported to a US-based divisional headquarters in Rhode Island, USA. This US connection was important to the formation of John Brown Automation. The US operation was involved not only in the machine tools business but also with automation equipment, for which North America was a small but relatively much more developed market than the UK.

Emerging automation opportunities in North America persuaded the John Brown Group of the long term potential of the domestic UK market. This encouraged it, when the decision was finally reached to dispose of Wickman Engineering, to retain its nascent automotive assembly capability in Coventry; hence the creation of John Brown Automation.

In the context of this background the position of John Brown Automation Ltd in 1983 was finely balanced. Immediately prior to its creation the automation operations were making losses, the unit possessed only a small number of employees who generated a minimal part of the John Brown Group turnover. Against this background the members of the new company recognised that progress was essential to survive. As is now well known, JBA went on to translate its initial slender opportunity into a success story. It has now become one of the UK's leading designers and builders of automated assembly systems and has a growing international reputation.

The Process of change

Three key steps were taken to set the company on its new course. These were the evaluation of opportunities, the creation of a strategy and putting the strategy into action.

Evaluation. Although there were signs of a developing automation market in North America, UK trends were much less clear. A number of considerations had to be taken into account, including the following. The automated assembly systems business was a specialist area. Also, there were no clearly identifiable UK market opportunities, so there was no discernible growth curve and market research and government statistics were unhelpful in evaluating the potential. Further, the business was something of a 'technological black art' requiring fresh thinking, new approaches and people capable of spanning several technical disciplines.

Strategic Direction. These considerations led the parent group to the conclusion that for the immediate future no detailed strategic growth and profitability objectives could be set. However, entering the market would need strict financial and administrative controls, in view of its potential for loss making. It was decided that the recruitment of a technically qualified management team, capable of pursuing the opportunity, was essential. In the absence of a clearly definable market opportunity the team would need the leadership of someone with specialist knowledge of the field.

Enactment. As a result of these decisions the following steps were taken. A target of a threefold increase in sales to £10 million by 1987 was set. JBA was also expected to attain an operating profit of 5 per cent of turnover.

New directors for sales, production, finance and technical support were recruited in the period 1983-86 (in one case by internal promotion) to provide a new top management team. A managing director was recruited externally. This appointment was finally made in 1984. The group had experienced some difficulty recruiting the right person, even though head hunters had been used. Furthermore, the creation of the top team over the period of 1983 to 1986 may appear to have been a more leisurely process than was the case.

The new company was given considerable autonomy by its parent company apart from the general operational targets for sales and profits and agreement on certain monitoring procedures. This may have been as a result of the specialist nature of the business, the troubles facing the parent group or the relative smallness of JBA within the overall group. Though the reasons remain unclear, the result has had a very positive effect on the attitudes of those running JBA. Management has been able to assume full responsibility and take decisions without going through long referral procedures. The autonomous relationship with the parent group has continued since the takeover by Trafalgar House.

Although operational autonomy has proved important to the speed with which progress has been achieved, support by the group has proved crucial in a number of ways, for the following reasons. As part of a larger group, rather than as a small company acting on its own, the company has been able to secure and underwrite the recruitment of the right calibre of leadership. The group was also able to finance the move to a new site. This was essential for the building and testing of extended automated assembly systems. The new premises also provided an opportunity to create a new identity and brought all employees together onto one site. The group was also able to underwrite a major contract which became available shortly after the creation of JBA, amounting to one third of the previous annual turnover. A similarly sized independent concern might well have had to decline such an increase in activity.

The Components of change

A number of practical, interrelated key steps were required to set the new company on its course. These included:

Market Orientation. A strategic move was made away from in-house manufacture of equipment and programmable controllers to the incorporation of other manufacturers' products in JBA systems . This enabled the company to move more quickly out of a relatively narrow product market niche into the broader-based opportunities of the market for the design, installation and commissioning of automated assembly systems.

In its formative days, when it manufactured its own products, JBA frequently found itself competing in a very limited market against the products of major international corporations such as Allen Bradley, Comau and Krause. In the absence of the support of Wickman Engineering this kind of competitive battle became difficult to sustain for the new company. In any case, some customers preferred the programmable logic controllers of other manufacturers for inclusion in equipment provided by John Brown Automation. In short, it was apparent that if the company were to tackle the automated systems market, it had to become market rather than product led, and adopt the philosophy of providing the customers with what they wanted.

This change, of course, had to be underpinned by the recruitment of new skills and specialist input, both of which were in short supply. This change in product skills effectively meant carefully managing the break up of a long established culture dominated by mechanical engineers and its replacement with another in which electronics and systems engineers played an equal part.

As a result, the company organised itself to offer a package of services rather than a group of products. This change in JBA's product and market strategies was complementary to general developments in the market, brought about partly by the growing availability of the 8 bit micro-processor. This facilitated the development of more sophisticated robotics and encouraged a growth of interest in flexible assembly systems. These trends were underpinned by the general need of much of British manufacturing to be 'fitter and leaner' which in turn encouraged the adoption of a 'Just in Time' approach to manufacturing efficiency to which automated assembly systems were seen by users as being well suited.

JIT and related developments, including early versions of the computerised materials requirements and production scheduling system, MRPII, required a systematic approach to the rationalisation of all aspects of the manufacturing process, rather than achieving productivity gains through islands of automation. Consequently JBA's move away from manufacturing into the design, building and commissioning of systems and solving systems problems was well matched to the changing needs of the market place. Nevertheless, JBA's experience, from its Wickman Engineering days, in the manufacture of machine tools continued to prove important.

The Development of Automated Assembly Systems. Since its foundation JBA has carried out a number of significant automation projects. These have included the provision of systems for automating the assembly of car engines, alternators, vehicle brakes, cylinder heads, door locks and electric motors. Recent achievements include the designing, building and commissioning of a 64 station automated car engine assembly line, a 21 station assembly line for power drills and an 11 station automated assembly line for domestic waste disposal units.

Some measure of the sophistication of the automated systems which JBA is creating can be gathered from the number of variants with which an automated car engine assembly line may deal: over 50 engine types, based on eight different blocks, four types of cylinder heads and different carburetters. Filters and ignition systems can be produced to suit a random production schedule delivering an engine every 45 seconds.

Automated assembly systems are, by their nature, dependent upon sophisticated computer systems to run them. This in turn calls for the use of advanced software and considerable programming skills in designing and building them. In a number of ways, therefore, the progress of JBA has reflected the use of computers in manufacturing over the last five years.

The increasing sophistication of programmable logic controllers (PLCs) from the late 1970s onward has enabled robotic machines to become independent of centralised computer processing capabilities. This development has resulted in the creation of more sophisticated automated linear assembly 'systems', as opposed to stand-alone robotic devices. The new PLCs heralded a very important market shift away from stand-alone automated assembly machines, the basis of the earlier Wickman business, to the development of automated assembly systems in which JBA's or other suppliers' machines could be incorporated. The world of computer-integrated manufacturing began to take shape in this period.

Integrated into such systems are computerised management information capabilities with built-in quality control and monitoring devices. These have helped place JBA at the leading edge of developments in the automated assembly systems business.

Organisational Mechanisms. The change of market and product emphasis required a new organisational approach. The company's new orientation towards systems required a broader base of technical expertise to understand both the systems and the individual machines. Expertise in understanding and designing the software required to make automative systems work, was especially important.

Work was previously organised around production processes. A new project-based system of working was introduced with teams composed of staff from the production, design office and electronic sections of the company. In order to ensure effective integration of the teams, a form of matrix management was introduced to enable employees to use their functional specialisations in electronics or design within the cross-functional project activities. By breaking the work up into discrete projects, management has been able to monitor and control activities more effectively. This became particularly important as the projects themselves increased in complexity and duration, sometimes taking up to two or more years.

One other important benefit of the project team approach has been the point of customer contact offered by the team and its leader. This has helped to provide customers with an assurance that their particular project is being given special attention, while enabling problems to be dealt with by the people directly involved.

As a result of these changes the company has been able to re-structure its organisation so that it has become both flatter and leaner. Intermediate lines of management have ceased to be required under the new project team based structure and certain functional responsibilities, for communications and personnel matters, have passed to line supervisors.

Planning and Operational Controls. The increasing complexity of JBA's automation projects have led to a recognition that the company's financial and administrative controls should reflect the increased complexities of its operation. From 1985 onward the company consolidated the following elements into its control programme.

The corporate plan looks short term and 3-5 years ahead, focuses on targets for turnover growth and sets out a productivity path showing expected annual improvements in net margins. The plan also deals with such issues as market segmentation (especially the development of opportunities in the other markets), geographical targets (ie in Europe and the USA) and acquisition policy.

The financial monitoring system is based on an evaluation of past performance. It is used to set budget targets and monitors achievements against goals.

Project progress is reviewed monthly or more frequently if the need arises. Monthly assessments are made of expenditure and time spent against project budgets and programme timetables. These reports are discussed with individual project teams in the presence of the managing director.

Technological Reinforcement. In recent years technological change has been extremely rapid. In the circumstances it has been difficult for many companies to keep pace with the changes. John Brown Automation, for its part, decided not to try to develop and run state of the art applications with their inherent uncertainties. They decided to remain at the leading edge of practical automated assembly applications. This approach influences customer philosophy as well as the company's internal processes. The company uses the latest technology, including advanced CAD and networking, to underpin marketing strategy. CAD was introduced in the early 80s. It has since been considerably enhanced to provide more efficient design production and to allow electronic exchange of design information between JBA and its customers.

Image. Another crucial step taken in the company's transformation process can best be described as an 'image' change. This was brought about by moving premises and by improving the company's marketing material.

In 1985 the company moved to new premises. These provided 60,000 sq ft overall and some 26,000 sq ft of clear assembly area in which to construct and test large automated systems. The move helped to confirm JBA as a serious player in the automated assembly business. It also enabled the company to create a separate identity for itself.

As part of the image change, promotional material was refocused, away from the things John Brown Automation could make, towards what the company's customers could make using John Brown automated assembly systems. This reflected a break with the strong cultural heritage in which the marketing effort had tended to emphasise the products that were made, rather than the market needs which they were capable of meeting. New promotional literature set out to reflect customer needs, as well as the high-tech calibre of support which the company could offer.

As a result of these changes the company has successfully repositioned its market image, emphasising the high-tech nature of its activities and its modern premises with smart promotional literature. The new name of John Brown Automation, symbolised its recently gained independence, as well as its new management.

Personnel implications

In carrying through its strategic reorganisation the company recognised the need for changes in its 'people' policies. A number of changes were made which included the following.

Creation of a Core Group of Employees. The inevitable gaps between the completion of one project and commencement of another exposed the company to possible periods of unprofitable under-utilisation of personnel. To reduce the potential difficulties, employment has been based on a core group of permanent employees. During peaks of activity the core group is supplemented by contract or part-time manpower, supplied by sub-contractors as the need arises. Sub-contractors are used to supply general labour needs but also carry out specific project work, such as wiring.

The company concentrates on building-up its essential core of skilled people, while using the part-time and contract workforce for less critical tasks. This approach has created a sense of elitism amongst employees which helps in recruiting and retaining high calibre personnel. However, these policies do not lead to difficulties in relations between the two groups. The length of project cycles is such that all employees are able to feel part of the project team.

Promotion of Individual Initiative. "It is the individual who counts. Our strength is in ourselves". This quotation sums up the company's belief in the importance of the individual to the company. Although employees work in project teams, the overall approach has been one of pushing decisions "down the line to the point of action" and to the individual concerned. This practice has raised the sense of responsibility of individual line managers as well as project team members. It is said to have helped to create an adaptable and flexible organisation capable of getting things done quickly.

To reinforce the creation of an individualistic environment a staff appraisal system was introduced in 1987 to enable individual performances to be monitored more effectively. The appraisal system now forms an integral part of the pay determination process. Pay is now determined by individual negotiation with line managers and not by collective bargaining as used to be the case. The responsibility of individual line managers has therefore been extended considerably to cover pay, individual assessments and communications. Line management training has been introduced to ensure that these new responsibilities are operated effectively.

Redefinition of the Role of Supervisory Management, the Personnel Function and Employee Representation. The process of creating personal initiative was reinforced by two important policy decision intended to strengthen the role and effectiveness of line management. The first was to delegate to them responsibility for the personnel function. At one time the company shared a personnel director with other parts of the John Brown Group, which provided a central personnel support service. JBA discontinued this practice with the aim of reinforcing the responsibility of line management for personnel matters. Administrative support, however, continues to be given by a personnel officer.

The second decision was that management should be responsible for communications with employees. JBA's former parent company, Wickman Engineering, had been unionised. However, after JBA was formed no formal arrangements were made to continue union recognition. The shop steward system which existed in the Wickman days continued to act as the information conduit between management and shop floor. However, in 1986, it was decided that this situation should be regularised and that line management should become responsible for all employee communications.

These policy changes threw up other important questions about the role of supervisory management. It was recognised that supervisors, as the interface with the shop floor, needed to have the skills to do this effectively. With this objective in mind, in 1986 the company introduced a supervisory management training programme.

Recruitment, skills and training. The company's change in activity from manufacturing to automated systems project management has required fundamental changes in the company's skills base. This has been brought about largely through a process of recruitment, but training initiatives have begun to play an increasing part in the change.

The skills shift has been appreciable. In 1986 there were some 30 engineers, of whom only 6 were electronic engineers. Now there are 50 engineers, 25 of whom are electronics specialists. These numbers reflect the growing sophistication of programmable devices and the increased need for enhanced software to take advantage of them.

The company is almost continuously recruiting graduate level engineers. In 1988 it had been taking on two graduate engineers per month for some time and planned to continue doing so. The workload had consistently run ahead of resources.

Recruitment has been seen as a positive way of changing the company's culture, by aiming at a new type of individual: described as "mechatronic, ambidextrous and adaptable". It would have been a considerable task for a small, growing company to train its own people and achieve the results it has. However, the company is now adopting new policies to make this possible.

During 1987 the company carried out a review of all training requirements with the encouragement of the Engineering Industry Training Board. Individual training profiles were drawn up. These training profiles have been matched to individual job experience matrices, with the intention of building in new experiences to promote personal development. The aim is to bring about total job involvement, particularly for engineers engaged on specialised projects.

On the shop floor, there are now intensive training facilities, including electrical courses, pneumatic courses for fitters and systems development personnel, supervisory courses and courses for project leaders. This increased effort is reflected in a training budget which was doubled in 1988 to £24,000 and of an apprenticeship scheme reintroduced in the same year.

Results

JBA made a loss of £300,000 in 1983. The company succeeded in becoming profitable in 1987, having increased turnover from £3m to £12.5m. In the same period direct employment doubled to 130 people. In addition there are significant numbers of contract employees.

JBA's financial success has been built by identifying a slender market opportunity for automated assembly systems, particularly in the motor vehicle industry. From this base the company has successfully expanded. This has required leadership, the adoption of new management and organisational approaches and the building-up of new skills. Not least, it has required the determination to re-orientate the company towards customer needs.

The company's growth and prosperity is striking because of its basis in the successful management of micro-electronic based technology and systems. Although John Brown Automation is still a relatively young and small company, its growth successfully reflects the rapid pace of change of information technology. It is interesting to reflect that this has been achieved in spite of the fact that, of all manufacturing operations, assembly operations are the most difficult to automate.

LEP GROUP AND LEP INTERNATIONAL

AWAKENING THE SLEEPING GIANT

The Group is the UK's best known freight forwarder. Lep International is its UK-based subsidiary.

Lep's difficulties in the early 1980s resulted in the recruitment of a new chief executive officer. The case study shows how leadership developed the talents of people at all levels, which resulted in all-round improvements in performance and increased profitability.

Background

In the late 1970s the employees of Lep International had grown accustomed to referring to their company as "the sleeping giant" of the freight forwarding industry. The process of "awakening" began in 1982, since when a radical transformation of the old-established firm has taken place.

Lep International is the freight forwarding arm of the Lep Group. Although this case study is mainly concerned with change in the former, it is inextricably linked with the radical development, since 1982, of the whole Group. The Lep Group now has a turnover of £1 billion, some 7000 employees and 250 offices world-wide, most of which are connected with the Group's international freight forwarding operations. Lep International is the UK arm of the Group's forwarding activities.

In 1986 the company made a profit of £1.11 million compared with a loss in 1981 of £369,000. In 1987 the company made a profit of £281,000 on a turnover of £212 million. However, the results in 1987 were affected by the acquisition of DBS Ltd, another important freight forwarder.

The freight forwarder nowadays acts as the agent for manufacturers and others, arranging the necessary transport, international documentation and customs clearance of products exported around the world. This can involve 24 hours per day real-time monitoring of the progress of an export order and the electronic interchange of information around the world. Inevitably, the fortunes of freight forwarders are linked to the international tide of export and import activity.

Lep International dates back to 1849, taking on something like its present identity in October 1910, when Lep Transport and Depository was incorporated. Over the years a number of offices were opened around the world but particularly in Europe where other forwarding firms were also acquired. These developments created a world-wide presence which enabled the company to provide an international service using either its own offices or its connections with other forwarding agents operating in other parts of the world.

The company was very successful and innovative. It was one of the earliest forwarders to use air freight, signing an exclusive air freight agency arrangement with Imperial Airways in 1924. At that time the company also handled 75 per cent of all UK motor imports and 50 per cent of all motor exports. Fifty years later the Company continued to show the same initiative, and was the first British company to gain a USA Air Couriers (Consolidators) Licence. By 1947, it became a public company, one of the few freight forwarders to do so, having built up a considerable reputation.

The Lep Group was built up by one man who joined the company in 1920 and who was managing director from 1930 until 1956 when he became chairman. He finally retired in 1972 and became Life President of the Lep Group until his death at the age of 92 in 1986. During this period the Life President's family became increasingly involved in making the Company a success, until by 1982 five of the nine directors of Lep Transport, were members of same family.

During the early 1980s Lep suffered from the downturn in international trade. Losses were incurred in Lep Transport in the years 1980 to 1982 while the Lep Group profits in 1982 fell to £475,000. At this juncture institutional shareholders decided that changes were necessary and a new chairman, a former senior partner in

Price Waterhouse, was appointed to run the Group.

The need for change

In 1982 there was some urgency in reversing the declining financial performance of the Group. There were also a number of external factors which were beginning to create pressure for change.

Among these was what has become known as "the globalisation of world markets". Manufacturing industry was rationalising, moving back to core businesses and cutting down on capital, tied up stocks and work in progress. Many companies which were used to carrying out their own forwarding operations cut back in their shipping departments in the interests of economy. They looked to forwarding agents to handle their export and import activities. In return, an efficient and cost-effective operation was required.

At the same time electronic technology was making the world seem smaller and electronic data interchange was increasingly being used for the international exchange of export and import information and documentation for transport, customs and payment purposes. All of these developments required adoption and Lep was not responding as quickly or as effectively as it had done in earlier years. Market share was lost to competitors. The industry had never been concentrated in the hands of a few major freight forwarders and even Lep's share was probably not much more than 10 per cent of the UK market. Also, the more rapid take-up of computer technology among foreign competitors enabled them to establish a foothold in the UK on which they have since built.

During this period Lep Group had no global strategy, although it provided a global service. The capability to get an export order from one side of the world to another did not amount to a policy to ensure survival. At home, Lep operated on the basis of a fragmented structure of branch offices, each one being allowed to compete with the others. In short, the Lep Group was in need of fundamental change and not just a restructuring of its financial performance.

The need for change applied particularly to the morale and attitudes of employees. These had become less than positive by the early 1980s. Lep had a strong reputation as a good employer among freight forwarders. It is thought to have been the first to have introduced (in 1930) a regular staff bulletin. The Group had many staff members with 20 and 30 year periods of service among its employees and these, to a great extent, helped to carry the business. However, by the early 1980s the majority of the talented employees had come to the conclusion that the way to the most senior positions was closed to them and that their skills were not being tapped.

The change programme

Leadership and Attitudes. The 1982 change of leadership in the Lep Group represented a considerable break with the past fifty years of family control. Employees in particular clearly saw the appointment as a start of a new era.

The new chairman saw that there were three basic possibilities for the Group: "tidy up and sell; fire everyone and recruit new management; and develop the existing resources, especially the people". It was the latter course he chose.

No strategy was ever set out on paper. There was no 'mission statement' sent out from the board or chairman's office. The new Chairman said: "The strategy was in my head". He saw his first task as one of "developing a concept and a strategy and keeping quiet about it". He realised that the Group had to fulfill people's needs for success but he also realised that some of the things which needed to be done could well require two steps forward and one backwards. The step backward could too easily be interpreted as failure. In addition, personal experience showed that the time involved in negotiating acquisitions could run to several years in some instances. It was recognised that patience had to be an essential part of the process of change.

The chairman acknowledged that his style of leadership was "a bit mysterious", with "an absence of big statements", but said that it was

built on a need for, and a deep belief in, a
respect of people. Objectives included
"changing attitudes from negative to positive",
"removing fear" and "being supportive of
people".

The new style of leadership has been open and
communicative, with the chairman getting
around the branches. The chairman believes
that "management owes it to people; they have
a contribution to make". As he has said, "so far
as I am concerned, if people have ability they
will be given a chance". Employees perceive
this to be the case: "the challenge has been
getting people to understand it doesn't matter
who they are but what they are capable of
doing".

The process of bringing people on has been
done with care, with people being promoted
slowly: "promote when people have a chance of
succeeding rather than failing". Challenges are
provided for employees, so as to develop them
for jobs they could be doing two years hence.
At the top level, Lep International Management, which now provides global co-ordination
for all Lep Group freight forwarding activities,
was established in 1986 as a natural progression
"when people were sufficiently developed to
take a policy forming role".

Giving priority to people-development has
resulted in the Group promoting from within,
in the main. This has helped reinforce the
expectations of employees: "there is nothing
worse than people being ignored". The process
of putting "people first" has enabled new
structures to be put in place without too much
apparent upheaval. The approach has sought
to build-in the considerable experience of the
Group's many long-serving employees.

Structural Changes. A new leadership style
and attitudinal changes from 1982 onwards
have underpinned a number of structural
changes in the Lep Group and, in particular,
Lep International. The changes are complex
and are interwoven, but fall roughly under the
following headings: decentralisation, rationalisation, diversification, integration, technological
integration, training and development and
consultation and communications.

Decentralisation. Until 1985 Lep Group and
Lep International occupied a prime site headquarters in Upper Thames Street in the City of
London where the Group had been located
since 1922.

The company vacated these premises, partly to
redevelop the site but also to enable the board
to decentralise operations, reduce headquarters' overheads and 'flatten' the management
structure.

New headquarters were established in Epsom,
accounting services were removed to Goole and
personnel and training were relocated to
Bromley. Staff numbers have been reduced
from 1981, when 1696 were employed, to 1285
people in 1987.

Rationalisation. The 1979-81 economic downturn had put freight forwarding margins under
considerable pressure during a period of
increased competition for business. Forwarding is in any case a high volume/low margin
operation, "a real nickel and dime" business
which requires careful monitoring and tight
controls.

Since 1982 the accounting function has been
continuously refined, with major changes in
cash management control being introduced in
1983-84. These involved more effective branch
budgeting procedures to enable operating
effectiveness to be properly monitored.

Diversification. The move of headquarters
from the City to Epsom enabled the Group to
capitalise on the development potential of its
former London base. This provided for a
significant improvement in the company's
financial standing and provided collateral of
£40 million for an acquisition programme to
strengthen the Group's position in markets
relevant to freight forwarding.

In 1985 Lep bought a UK-wide transport and
warehousing company, Swift Transport. Swift
remains an independently managed part of
LEP, but co-operation between the two
operations has grown and is being further
developed.

In 1987 Lep made a major North American acquisition, taking over the freighting and warehousing business, Profit Systems, with a turnover of $138 million and 1000 employees in 60 offices around the United States including Canada and Puerto Rico. Profit Systems is providing opportunities in the North American market, as well as a natural bridge to the Pacific markets. Profit Systems has built up a strong reputation for reliability in the 'time definite' delivery business and helped to meet the growing demand in the UK for this kind of international service.

Other diversifications have been made by the group outside its main stream freight forwarding activities; in warehouse security protection, with an interest (now a 40.6 per cent holding) acquired in 1984 in an American firm, National Guardian Company, which is involved in the distribution of bearings and power transmission products; in insurance broking operations; and in property. All of these operations have natural connections with Lep's traditional forwarding operations.

Lep makes the point that these diversifications are easy to conceptualise but take considerable time to negotiate to a satisfactory conclusion. Acquiring Profit Systems took three years from start to finish.

Integration. The last six years have seen a number of steps taken which have aimed to make Lep a more unified force in the forwarding world, both at home and abroad, as well as in air and surface freighting services.

Branches, in the UK and internationally, tended in the past to operate as autonomous units, in competition with one another. In an increasingly globalised business, this was thought to be self defeating. Large multi-plant manufacturing businesses expected some kind of integrated national service and multinational companies expected similar global services where international transactions were concerned.

In 1985 Lep combined its two main forwarding operations, Lep Transport, which dealt with surface forwarding, and Lep Air which dealt with air forwarding, into one unit called Lep Air.

At the same time a new slogan was created, 'The New Way Forward' and a new logo and house style was developed. Lep forwarding therefore underwent an important image change, which was seen as an essential step in underscoring its integration both within the UK and internationally.

The international integration process was strengthened through the acquisition of a number of well known forwarding operations: Storintex in Holland; Munditrans in Spain; Breinholt in Sweden; Gheng SA, a long established French forwarding group; and Luvigsa in Peru. These, together with Profit Systems greatly strengthened Lep's international forwarding operations, especially in its two most important markets, Europe and the USA.

Diversification was also extended to Lep's forwarding operations. For some time a certain amount of consolidation of freight, both air and deep sea, had been undertaken by specialist 'consolidators'. These provided a cheaper form of freight movement by buying bulk container space and selling it out in 'parcel lots', acting rather as a wholesaler. Lep has extended its operations in this area and set up a National Consolidation Unit specialising in deep sea surface cargo, having been in the air cargo consolidation business for many years.

The organisational unification of freight forwarding was taken further in 1986 with the creation of LIM, Lep International Management, to oversee Lep's international freight forwarding operations and provide a common policy framework. LIM is composed of the heads of forwarding operations around the world, the UK being represented by the managing director of Lep International, the biggest of all the units in terms of turnover and employees.

Another interesting step was the introduction of portfolio responsibilities for directors so that they cover both functional line management and market responsibilities. In this way directors hold line responsibility for different regions of the UK and functional responsibility for areas of overseas development. The sales and marketing director also provides line responsibility for special services, such as the transportation of racehorses around the country. There are no finance, information technology or personnel directors, although managers for the first two of these functions, together with the directors, form the management team.

Technological integration. The modern world of freight forwarding is wholly dependent on electronic data interchange. It is said that "Lep would be dead without information technology". Lep has 500 terminals on line connecting its branch structure, providing control over its forwarding operations and accounting, marketing and management information.

This system, called Lepnet, was introduced in 1978 and has been developed further since then. It helps provide coverage of all aspects of the international movement of cargo: imports and exports, air freight, overland, short and deep sea.

The globalisation of Lep's services has put this system under increasing pressure. Installations around the world have tended to take place on a local basis, without having to pay too much regard to communication protocols with other software and hardware systems. This is an approach adopted by many multinational concerns and it is one that has resulted in a proliferation of different types of installation. In Lep's case there are some dozen different systems worldwide.

Lep has taken steps to rationalise and integrate its IT capability and, in 1987, appointed an IT manager, to provide support for this operation. Trials with a new system called 'Lilian' (Lep International Links in a Network) have been running for more than a year in the Far East, Germany and Canada. Wherever necessary, Lep has upgraded its old system to cope with increasing volumes of business until 'Lilian' is fully operational.

The purpose of these technological changes is to provide an integrated international service, but to enable this to be done with fewer employees. In addition, tighter operational monitoring of branch performance will become possible, while at the same time branch performance is being improved through more effective interchange of information about market opportunities.

Training developments. Training has also been subjected to review during the period since 1982, although the company was said to have been a noted exception among forwarders in carrying out some training before then. A National Training Manager was appointed in 1985 to provide a central support service to the branches. Each branch has a training budget, although it is left to local discretion as to how and where this should be spent.

Training courses are run on the practical aspects of freight forwarding, such as the handling of dangerous goods, Customs and Excise requirements and the like. However, the emphasis has been steadily moved towards the broader development of people, rather than just the improvement of their effectiveness in their own jobs. This is said to be partly a reflection of the directors' support for training and partly a response to improved attitudes among employees, who are keener to develop themselves. Whatever the reasons, the training team has been strengthened and now has four staff, two of whom specialise in the training for computer skills.

Lep was among the first forwarders to introduce a management training programme. One of the joint managing directors appointed to run Lep International in 1982 when the new chairman took up his post was a product of the programme. The old scheme was based on the recruitment of graduates who were then taken through the 'fast-track' programme. The system had come to be regarded as a divisive: "the graduates were treated as gods". A new scheme is to provide management training for anyone judged capable of being a manager, as well as for graduate recruits. The company considers that it "has a remarkable number of above average performers". The new scheme is designed to give all employees, most of whom were early school leavers, a chance to develop. Those who continued their education and came into the company having gained their formal qualifications are treated equally.

Consultations and communications. The change process in Lep has been facilitated by the use of a consultant reporting personally to the chairman. The consultant has been used from time to time to ascertain the views of particular groups of employees or individuals and advise the chairman on courses of action, appointments, problems and opportunities.

In other respects the process of change has been handled internally, mainly through the formation of working parties to review particular issues. These are few in number; at the moment there are three dealing with information technology, 1992 and the Channel Tunnel, and market opportunities.

Forwarding, in Lep, is regarded as a network business with branches providing regular customer contact, supported by a small head quarters staff. It is said to be a simple business and the motto is "keep it bloody simple". Consequently the change process has been kept as straightforward as possible, with the separation of the activities of policy formation from the day to day operations. However, the daily round of intensive communication between branches and HQ, which is a necessary feature of international forwarding, makes for a considerable informal network of communication and contact. In this way a good deal of feedback is provided on virtually all aspects of the business. This process of exchange is reinforced by regular visits to branches by the chairman, the managing director and the directors with regional responsibilities.

Because of the volume of informal communication, there has been some ambivalence about formal structures, such as briefing meetings. These were introduced in 1986 but then faded away. Some branch managers continue to hold meetings and a new company-wide system has been considered and will be introduced.

Lep International also started (1987) to bring all its managers together for regular meetings. The exact form of these, how many and down to what level they should be involved, is undergoing review.

Customer communications are also being reconsidered. A regular newsletter is being issued to all clients.

The results

The effect of all the changes that have taken place has been to make Lep International more profitable and more competitive. As mentioned at the beginning, in 1981 the company made a loss of £369,000 million which it turned into a net profit of £1.11 million in 1986. The Lep Group, for its part, has turned its 1982 net profit of £475,000 into a 1988 net profit of £6.5 million.

Overall the changes since 1982 can be summed up as: new leadership, a new decentralised and diversified structure, an integrated international service, a new name and image, new attitudes, improved morale - it is said that "we want people to come to work whistling" - and increased collective commitment to succeed. There is certainly a combined sense of certainty that the company will continue to make considerable progress.

LUCAS INDUSTRIES

THE SYSTEMS ENGINEERING APPROACH

Lucas Car Braking Systems in Pontypool and in Bouzonville, France, illustrate a systematic approach to the reorganisation of production processes, following an analysis of the competitive gap that had to be bridged to enable both plants to assume leadership in their respective markets.

The case studies describe how Competitive Achievement Plans (CAP), and manufacturing systems engineering methodology, were used to reverse poor performance in both Pontypool and Bouzonville. The drive for change came from Lucas Industries' review of operations, following its first ever loss in 1981. The stimulus to unit-level review of the engineering methodology and training was developed from the centre. Both plants have a high level of union membership.

The case studies are excellent examples of how companies can raise performance by making better use of existing resources. The productivity gains achieved are said by Lucas to be only 30 per cent attributable to investment in technology and 70 per cent to improvements in manufacturing systems methodology.

A Strategy For Change

The structure of this case study differs from others in the series. It is actually a composite of three partial studies of the management of change, at two levels of a major organisation employing over 50,000 people in more than 100 operating units. The first part outlines the central features of the Lucas Group's strategic approach. The rest looks at the actual implementation of that approach in two of the Group's operating units, Lucas Car Braking Systems at Pontypool in South Wales and at Bouzonville in France. During most of the period covered the units formed part of Lucas Girling and, where appropriate, this name is used in the case study.

There are two reasons for adopting this composite structure. First, from the company's point of view, this is an integrated change strategy, in the sense that the group has developed it, encourages units to apply it, and makes available the resources to enable them to do so. The management of change at Pontypool and Bouzonville can only be understood in the light of guidelines laid down at group level; likewise, the effectiveness of Lucas' strategic approach can only be assessed at unit level.

Second, this structure may be helpful from the point of view of the readers, many of whom will be operating at one or other level in a similar group/unit relationship. Recent management literature has included several examinations of the actual and proper strategic role of group HQs in relation to their constituent units. Some have come up with typologies of group approaches, eg "Targeting - Guiding - Directing - Running HQs"[*] and of perceived HQ roles, eg "Controller - Coach - Orchestrator - Surgeon - Architect HQs".[**]

Although the group/unit aspects of this case study are of interest, the essence of the Lucas approach is its carefully thought through mechanism for designing products and manufacturing systems in ways which satisfy market needs.

Background

Founded in 1886, Lucas became a major supplier of components and systems to a wide variety of industries, but especially to the domestic UK automotive industry. As a consequence of its major customers' fast decreasing competitiveness and loss of market shares in the late 1970s, Lucas made its first operating loss in 1981. This sparked off a major programme of plant closures and job losses.

Going into the red also caused Lucas to recognise that "maintaining the system" was no longer good enough, and that a radically new, strategic approach to all its businesses would be required in order to regain competitiveness. Over the next two years, they introduced a number of key innovations (each of which figure in the Unit case studies, below).

---

*CRESAP, "The Effective HQ", BIM 1988.
**Signed Reinton and Nationiel Foote, Financial Times 17/6/88, drawing on Michael Goold and Andrew Campbell, "Strategies and Styles", Basil Blackwell 1987.

Introducing Competitiveness Achievement Plans

Lucas began by requiring each of its (approximately) 140 units to produce a Competitiveness Achievement Plan (CAP) to prove that the unit had a vision of where it needed to get to, and a plan for getting there. Each unit was required to identify its most effective international competitor, outline the competitor's performance and, if the unit was being out performed, to spell out in detail how and when the gap could be closed and what would be the financial and other support needed from the group to make it happen.

Units whose CAPs failed to persuade the group that they offered a realistic chance of regaining competitiveness were not retained. But even the successful CAPs highlighted the fact that, across the group as a whole, a major stumbling-block was the general absence of a coherent manufacturing strategy. The group looked outside and appointed a new group director of manufacturing technology, to devise one.

His analysis was that the company's manufacturing capability was fundamentally handicapped by inadequate professional development in many functions, an outdated technician culture in production, and ineffective manufacturing systems in general. The latter had been adequate for the business of 20 years ago: relatively few products, produced in high volumes using highly specialised equipment and supported by people at all levels with narrowly-defined work tasks. They were quite inappropriate to modern requirements for high product variety, produced in lower volumes to consistent standards of quality, through the use of highly flexible manufacturing systems supported by equally flexible people.

The Systems Engineering Approach

The strategic need was therefore to develop an approach to systems engineering, embracing business systems engineering and manufacturing systems engineering, applied to both the organisation of manufacturing processes and to manpower. The overall objective, which became the responsibility of Lucas Engineering and Systems, was "to recreate simplicity through systematic professional design". The underlying philosophy saw innovation as a blend of improvements in technology and methodology, with the latter likely to provide 70 per cent of the benefit. The inherent barriers to a systems approach were occupational specialisms generated by the pattern of engineering education and set in fragmented and complex organisation structures.

As in 1983 the systems engineering concept was so unfamiliar in UK manufacturing that Lucas had to begin by developing its own modular training programme. The group's central training department was heavily involved in this development, there being little available "off the shelf" outside. In order to gain commitment and to demonstrate to everyone the importance being attached to systems engineering, a "top-down" training programme was decided upon.

Board members received their awareness training first, then all general managers, followed by all senior managers, and so on, over two years. A large amount of retraining and updating was found to be required. All managers had to learn new ways of operating and new organisational styles. The decision to opt for methodology, rather than technology, was certainly not the cheap, easy option.

Having developed the systems engineering approach, the next step was to apply it, in order to reorganise the manufacturing process, often completely, in virtually every one of the units which survived after the initial CAP appraisal. This required the establishment of new mechanisms at group and unit levels.

Task forces

The key unit-level mechanism is the Task Force, the remit of which is first to review, and then to change the Unit's manufacturing organisation. The Task Force brings together people from different functions within the unit, including marketing, finance, design, personnel and product and manufacturing systems engineering to analyse and solve their own unit's problems. Most Task Forces have 4-6 members. So far, over 100 have been formed.

The unit's management team is first trained as a mixed-skill group. They then choose the members of their Task Force and, with the help of Lucas Engineering and Systems Ltd (see below), train them and work with them to set competitive business targets. The Task Force then works full-time, usually for 4 to 6 months, on a business redesign project.

Task Forces are guided in their analysis by the structured, total strategy approach which Lucas has developed, which starts with a detailed definition of marketing strategy. The process of manufacturing business redesign which Lucas has developed has five basic steps or strategic components, under the general umbrella of a total quality programme approach.

• Business and Marketing Strategy: Examine all data on markets, competitors and factory processes, to see where you stand, decide what to make and what to buy-in and define target business ratios to match the world leader.

• Product and Manufacturing Systems Engineering Strategy: Do an engineering value-added analysis of all processes and supporting functions to define product groups and eliminate no-value-added activities. Techniques such as process flow analysis and group tech-nology allow definition of self-contained cell structures operable by teams).

• Business Systems Engineering Strategy: Design for each cellular business unit a simpler integrated organisation structure, with cellular project units, more flexible, simpler job struc-tures and measures of performance reflecting the target business ratios.

• Information Systems Strategy: Design the information flow and adjust the business system design to make the business organisa-tion structure and information systems compatible and controllable with maximum simplicity.

• Financial Strategy: Adjust to allow for dynamics and integrate all systems, controls and organisational processes with financial strategy. Provide a business justification for the change.

If the business general manager accepts that the Task Force's project proposal is viable, implementation begins. Completion may take 3 years, or even longer, depending on the complexity of the changes to be tackled. These changes may affect processes, procedures, organisation and job content. The speed of change may be affected by the ability of local management, the calibre of the Task Force and the judgement of unit managers as to the proper pace of change. During this time the Task Force reports to the business unit manager, who is effectively its customer and sponsor.

Developing change from the centre

Expert help is available to Task Forces through Lucas Engineering and Systems. This company has a systems engineering contracting unit which employs about 140 younger graduate manufacturing systems engineers and business systems engineers, many of whom have been developed as generalist engineers through courses developed by the Lucas Group. In many cases, Lucas Engineering and Systems staff have taken the Integrated Graduate Development Scheme (IGDS) run by Warwick University's Department of Engineering. IGDS provides a part-time 3-year, modular Master's course in Manfucturing Systems Engineering, jointly developed with, and taught by Warwick University and the staff of 25 participating companies. The scheme is headed by the University's Lucas Professor of Manufacturing Systems Engineering. Lucas has also supported six other chairs in other universities and polytechnics.

Lucas Engineering and Systems' role in Task Forces is to provide the systems engineering expertise and to help with the introductory training of the Task Force members. They are involved on a straight forward commercial contract basis by invitation. The Lucas Engineering and Systems engineers are subcon-tractors who work as members of the Task Force. They offer help on "how to do it" as well as what needs to be done; for example, by helping to develop the use of analytical tech-niques, or by assistance in conducting a skills audit. The working relationship may become so productive that Lucas Engineering and

LUCAS AUTOMOTIVE - OBJECTIVES

- To be a major supplier of systems and components in our chosen technologies

- To be regarded by the Automotive industry internationally as an adaptable, reliable and competitive supplier offering good and consistent value to customers - both original equipment and aftermarket

- To achieve and maintain international competitiveness throughout the Company with particular emphasis on product reliability and performance, product cost and service support

- To achieve target financial criteria consistently, and to generate sufficient funds to meet commitments and to support required investments

- To raise the standards of performance in a "total quality organisation" by encouraging creativity and innovation and by developing a competent, committed and fully motiviated team

Both manufacturing units involved in this study belong to one of Lucas Industries' main subsidiaries, Lucas Automotive and specialise in the manufacture of brakes.

Lucas Automotive was created by a corporate reorganisation at the end of 1987. It covers more than 40 business units, grouped into seven divisions: Lucas Heavy Duty Braking Systems, Lucas Car Braking Systems, Lucas Diesel Systems, Lucas Electrical Products, Lucas Engine Management Systems, Lucas Body Systems and Lucas Aftermarket Operations. In 1987, Lucas Automotive accounted for two-thirds of Lucas Industries' £1.8bn turnover. Its strategic objectives, as defined by the Managing Director, are set out in Figure 1.

Lucas Car Braking Systems has a world-wide network of units involved in the development and manufacturing of a variety of brake products, including high-technology anti-skid systems. Four of those units are located in Europe: Koblenz (West Germany), Pamplona (Spain), Pontypool (South Wales) and Bouzonville (France). Their main products are outlined in Figure 2. Ford, VW/Audi and Renault together account for half of the sales.

This case study covers the plants at Pontypool and Bouzonville. Pontypool manufactures a wider range of product families while Bouzonville manufactures a wide variety of products within its single product family: disc brakes. However, there are also similarities between Pontypool and Bouzonville, which guided their choice for this study. Both currently employ about 1,000 people and they have similar occupational/skill profiles. Both have sales of about £60m a year. At the time of the initiation of the CAP exercise, both were loss-making; neither now is.

But this is not a comparative study of the adoption of the systems engineering approach. The Pontypool report focuses on the development of the factory's management organisation structure and its impact on supervisory work. The Bouzonville report concentrates more on the Task Force's analysis of the required physical rearrangement of the plant, Lucas Engineering and Systems' role in that, and the wider effects on job content and training needs.

JULY 1984

LUCAS GIRLING LIMITED

PONTYPOOL

TERMS OF REFERENCE

SCS PROJECT TEAM

- To review the current project commitments to SCS manufacture and design a practical competitive manufacturing system embodying best proven principles, new working practices, flexibility and (via simplification of system design) eliminate the need for major indirect support.

- To provide a module layout to correspond with the above and provide basic designs for local bottom up systems including on-line real-time WIP control procedures.

- To include manufacture of SCS modulator, SCS valve and the machining of the Power Servo, Valve Block and Manifold Block.

- To identify opportunities for automation in handling, kitting and assembly.

LUCAS CAR BRAKING SYSTEMS, PONTYPOOL

In 1983 the long established Pontypool factory was losing money heavily. It was then subjected to two external pressures which sparked off a major reorganisation of its business. The first pressure came from the Lucas Group, and the second from a major customer.

Lucas' request for Pontypool's Competitive Achievement Plan (CAP) forced into the open a number of long-standing operating problems. By European standards the factory had low productivity, high costs of quality, an unsatisfactory performance in meeting delivery dates and poor industrial relations, with high absenteeism. As in other factories, formulating the CAP also exposed an indifferent ability to analyse the fundamental reasons.

At about the same time, Ford was exploring the possibility of placing a contract for the manufacture of Lucas's Stop Control System (SCS) for the Escort car. SCS would be Pontypool's first genuinely new product for many years; a guarantee of its future and a major feather in Pontypool's cap. They were determined to make a success of the new product and the General Manager welcomed the opportunity for fundamental change provided by the CAP process and manufacturing systems engineering methodology.

The change process

After local management had reviewed best manufacturing practice in Germany and Japan, terms of reference were drawn up for a full-time "SCS Project Team" (Task Force) - see Figure 3. Five months later the Task Force presented its feasibility study report, containing detailed proposals for a modern manufacturing unit. The proposals were accepted, and implementation began in January 1985. Manufacturing systems engineering methodology was employed, and Lucas Engineering and Systems was involved. A key feature of these proposals was that SCS manufacturing would effectively become a separate business run by an integrated team: a "factory within a factory".

As a result, further Task Forces were set up on the same site during 1985 to carry out redesign feasibility studies of the manufacture of disc brake and actuation products. They worked for seven months, and both produced recommendations for a far-reaching reorganisation of production facilities. The company executive sanctioned the required investment, and the implementation process began in April and August of 1986, respectively.

It became increasingly clear that the factory's organisation structure was a major impediment to Pontypool's ability to maximise the benefits of these changes. In mid-1986 it displayed all the classic rigidities to which the Lucas Systems and Engineering approach had been addressed; functionally separate, pyramidally-shaped, with many layers of management. There was a complicated structure of management, (all managers reporting to the factory manager), superintendents, general foremen and foremen. For example, the span of control of (for example) a Superintendent was always vertical, down to production workers and never horizontal, across to engineering and other functions. The structure made good managers ineffective, and made the factory almost impossible to manage.

The general manager decided to "go for accountability" and replace these ineffective structures by three discrete manufacturing businesses: SCS; Disc Brakes; and Actuation, plus a fourth, Site Services Business. Each manufacturing business would be run by a manufacturing manager, reporting to the factory manager and supported by a dedicated, multi-functional team including technical support (industrial, quality and reliability engineers, etc) and supplies support (eg manufacturing controllers).

Each would therefore be semi-autonomous and responsible for virtually the whole range of activities necessary to produce the product family: machining, assembly, industrial engineering, quality and materials supply, and maintenance. The exceptions to total business accountability were functions such as sales and marketing, accounts and invoicing, product engineering and personnel, which were

LUCAS FIGURE 4:

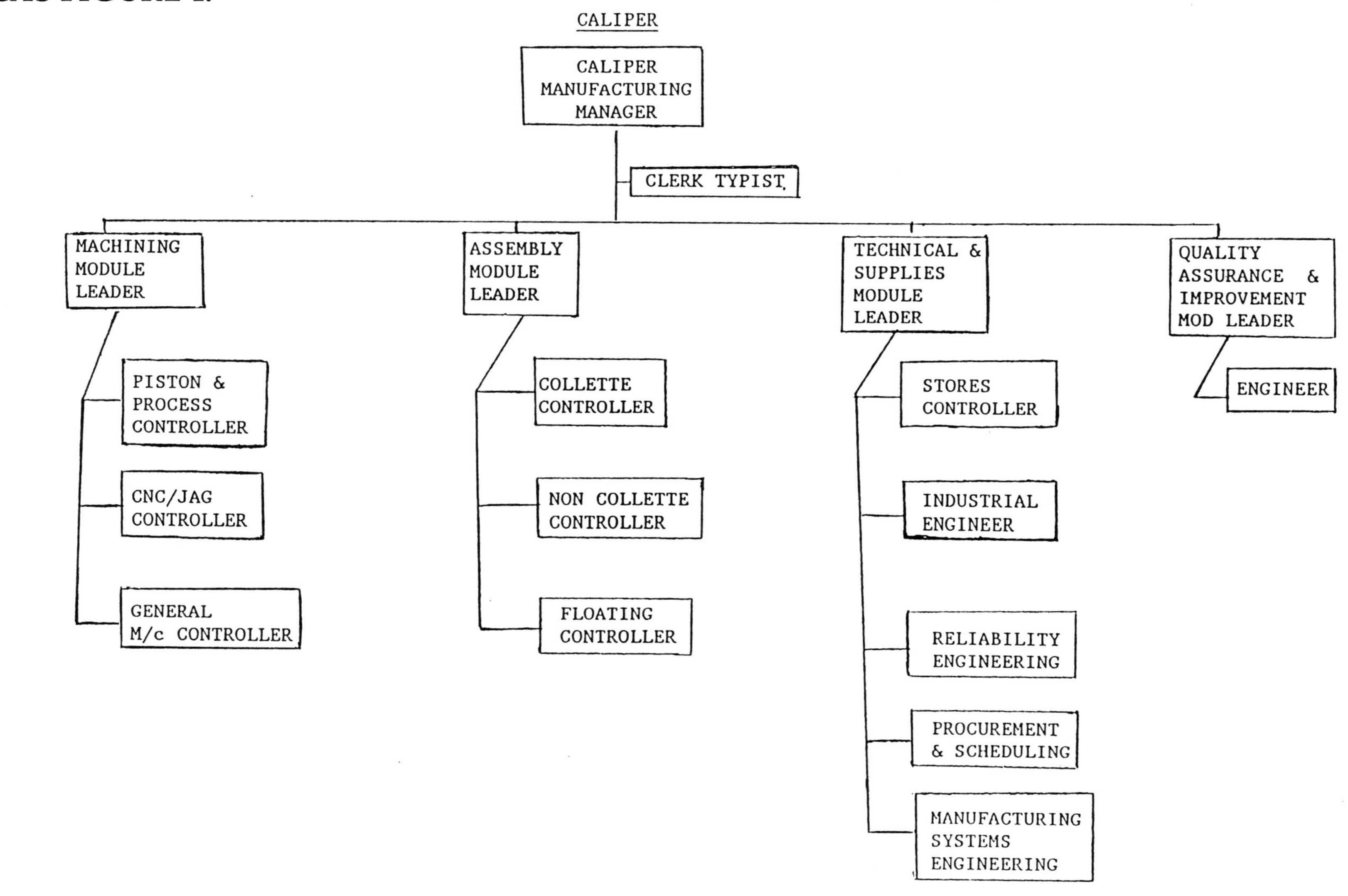

site-based for cost-effectiveness, and the tool-room, located as a contracting business involved in its ownright within site services.

The site management team, all of whom were given training in manufacturing systems engineering principles, held an off-site brain-storming exercise to determine a management structure for each separate business. The aim was, by making them manageable, to achieve the aims of accountability and reliability. They decided upon a two-tier structure of activity-based product modules managed by module leaders and units managed by unit controllers. Figure 4 shows this structure for the caliper (disc brake) business.

Pontypool management saw the key objective of the Business/Module/Unit approach as being to introduce purpose-designed manufacturing units with a high degree of autonomy and defined lines of accountability. The changes to be made would include:

• dedicated stores;

• Kanban material flow control;

• stand-alone scheduling, procurement and planning,

• production to be responsible for quality, using statistical process control techniques;

• allocation of production and works engineers to the discrete manufacturing businesses.

The customer would see the benefit in terms of faster response to schedule changes, improved delivery performance and "zero defect" quality. The factory would become manageable.

THE PROSPECT OF CHANGE IN MANAGEMENT

The change appears to have been beneficial at all levels. The factory manager's task was no longer absolutely impossible. By delegating some of his tasks to the businesses, the reorganisation made room for him to focus more clearly both on the factory's key operational objectives. These included the achievement of European levels of competitiveness, implementing matrix management for the introduction of all new production and intensifying essential training and retraining programmes. More strategically they aimed to widen the customer and supplier base, achieving volume goals and seek new product introductions.

Changes in responsibility. The business manager's job in the caliper business had no equivalent within the old structure. The current manager came into the job from one of the functional hierarchies, saw his role as an enabling role, and worked through the four module leaders and 13 unit controllers (including 2 "floating" controllers) to achieve: "management at the lowest possible level".

The development of this more 'bottom-up' management style owes much of its success to top management's own commitment. Much greater accountability, the word on every manager's lips, has been achieved in the caliper business by the proximity of the management team to its 340 people; this also "creates a happier family atmosphere which is beginning to soften traditional attitudes". Organisational change is felt to have had a greater impact on the volume and quality of output than the £2.5m. capital investment programme which preceded it: "now we always achieve our monthly production budget. Before 1987 we never did".

The closest analogue to the Module Leader in the old structure was the supervisor. Some supervisors moved into the new posts but there the similarities ended. The module leader's role was far wider, involving all aspects of production instead of one function. And within that wider role, greater responsibility was introduced: "I now manage totally... I have a free hand, focusing on a smaller area of the factory but in far greater detail". Forward planning was much enhanced and the former "fire fighting 24 hours a day with your hands tied" has been almost eliminated. Day-to-day problems became easier to solve for three reasons. First, because a cross-functional team of people was on tap, instead of having to prise a specialist out of some separate hierarchy and

LUCAS FIGURE 5:

TOTAL QUALITY ORGANISATION

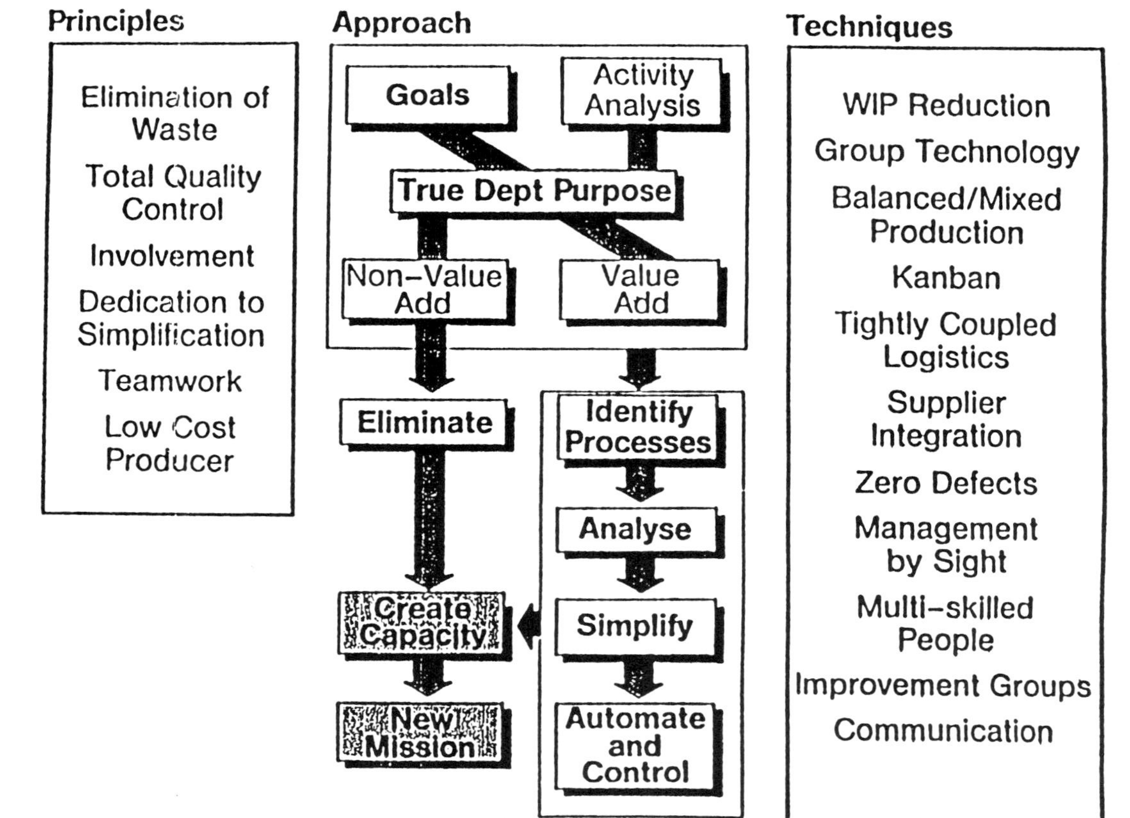

location. Second, information flows were improved, which meant that "I now know when there's a supplier problem, so I can plan for it". Third, the new arrangements were felt to be encouraging more co-operative attitudes on the shop floor.

Changing roles. Making the transition was not plain sailing. Accountability brought new pressures, and "the change was a shock for a while. It didn't look like a good move at first". Even having become convinced of the correctness of the new structures, "the hard thing is to convince the rest of the people in the module that what we're doing is right for them and right for the business". But overall, the module controller's job became "easier, more challenging and a lot more satisfying. Improvements are noticeable, ...and they are 70 per cent down to better methodology".

Several former foremen filled the new unit controller posts. The managerial scope of the job became narrower, in the sense that the controller was responsible for managing fewer people, (though this will change, with the forecast increase in direct staffing). However, the role became very different, "I was a taskmaster, now I'm a co-ordinator", as did the day-to-day content of the job, with a lot more emphasis on planning and a lot less on firefighting.

The most visible change has been the development of team working: "I used to feel isolated, trying to persuade people from other departments - especially engineers - to give me some service. After a while, you think the team, and everybody's interested. People just get on with the job if I'm not around".

Personnel policies to support change

The Lucas approach recognises that reorganisation and restructuring per se will not maximise required improvements in productivity, quality and on-time delivery (though, as can be seen, it can immediately improve these indicators). The approach also recognises the need to back up changes with a major effort of training and retraining, and other personnel policies. But the Lucas Systems and Engineering approach deliberately leaves these enabling mechanisms for determination at local level, although a

personnel consultancy capability can be provided.

Pontypool has introduced a number of policies to help make its various Task Force recommendations effective.

Reorganising the factory called for restructuring the jobs of direct workers. The 'mould-breaking' SCS reorganisation presented an opportunity to negotiate change, because the employees and their representatives knew both how critical the new product was to the factory, and how close they had come to losing it.

The SCS Task Force worked out the main job restructuring requirements. They were then included in a video presentation about the new business. Six distinct SCS production jobs were identified: two craft jobs (with responsibility for training others); two machine controller jobs; assembler/tester; and materials controller. In addition, the Task Force identified certain tasks common to all:

• carrying out minor maintenance tasks and elementary routine preventative maintenance;

• standing in, as required, on other jobs within the SCS Business which were considered "within competence";

• participation in such activities as Improvement Teams;

• carrying out statistical process control measurement.

While these were radical proposals, the trade unions indicated they would not oppose them, provided the necessary training was given. This early success was later applied to jobs in the other businesses. As one manager observed, "that agreement helped us across a lot of barriers".

Training for change. Pontypool management did, and does, recognise the importance of a consistent, supporting training programme plan, designed to enhance skills, develop flexibility and increase motivation. The SCS reorganisation involved an average of five week's formal training per employee. Again, the Task Force (which in this case included a

Training Officer) was able to point the way forward, by producing a detailed matrix of the basic types of skills and knowledge essential to each job, from the business manager down. Each cell team member, including the leader, was provided with a personal training plan.

Training provision increased significantly. In 1984, the factory training department supplied 16,000 trainee hours; just under 1 per cent of working time. By 1987 that number had doubled, and 1988 saw a further increase. To help cope with the demand an open learning unit had been set up in mid-1987 with more than 50 job-centre training packages. Most were developed by Lucas Central Training Department in collaboration with Lucas Engineering and Systems engineers and managers. The unit is open 8 hours a day. Its time is allocated to the businesses, and the utilisation level is over 80 per cent. Interest is such that business managers complain about their allocation of time.

The volume of this essential change-related training was planned to continue to increase. The new Pontypool emphasis was placed on developing a more strategic approach to training, clearly related to the business strategy. That approach emphasised: the achievement of training standards as a requirement for progression; an increased professional training capability; the need to develop trainers within the businesses, as well as at the centre; and more emphasis on monitoring the quality, efficiency and effectiveness of training provision which had grown so that it accounted for about 2 per cent of contracted working time.

Rationalisation of rewards. It was recognised that the structure of the rewards package also needed to support restructuring elsewhere in the system: Pontypool replaced the original 11 grade pay structure for manual workers with a 4-grade structure. Bonus payments were designed to mirror the key business objectives of improved productivity, delivery, absenteeism and quality.

Pontypool management recognised that these improvements had as much to do with attitudes as with skills and organisational structures. They decided that systematic attention to employee communication and involvement practices could do a great deal to help change attitudes. There was also seen to be a need for management to work more directly with their staff, rather than simply through representative arrangements.

Communications and Involvement. A number of initiatives were introduced, as part of both a general review of practices in this important area, and a "Total Quality Organisation" programme (see Figure 5). A factory-wide initiative to introduce "Communication Meetings" based on natural cell team groups got under way in late 1987. As an example of the new approach, the caliper business stopped production for about 15 minutes on a weekly basis (or more frequently, as necessary), to brief everyone on key issues concerning production matters, performance against targets, personnel matters (such as absence trends), customer visits, and so on.

In addition to team briefing, communications mechanisms include:

• factory noticeboards

• communications noticeboards, (one in each module)

• the factory magazine

• audio-visual presentations of business trends and prospects

• meetings of senior stewards with the factory manager (on a weekly basis), with the business managers (on a weekly basis) and with the site general manager (on a monthly basis)

• monthly supervisory policy meeting.

In addition, in late 1987 quality circles (or improvement groups) were introduced generating considerable interest from the shop floor. By the spring of 1988 eight groups had been formed and a full time facilitator had been appointed. The creation of these groups had hitherto been held back by the need to secure improvements to the communication structure.

In all these (and other) personnel areas, Pontypool has done a good deal but recognises that more needs to be done to ensure that its policies and practices do not lag behind and thereby constrain the effectiveness of other changes in the business. As one manager put it, "technological change is no great problem. Shifting round the machinery is easy. Getting people to work flexibly is the key to successful change, and we need to be on top of policies which can contribute to that".

How much progress?

An objective review of progress, carried out early in 1988, concluded that while there remained potential for further involvement, much had been accomplished. It was said that: "We match European best in a number of business sectors; in product innovation, new product introduction, supply performance, quality performance, employee flexibility and growth business with important customers. Matching European best productivity levels more generally would be achieved in 1988, as the full implementation of improvement programmes is completed. A culture of continuous improvement is rapidly gaining ground".

It seemed clear that the Lucas Engineering and Systems approach has played a significant enabling role. The CAP requirement had the kind of major shock effect so often necessary to provoke a fundamental reassessment, as a preliminary to radical change. The manufacturing systems engineering methodology provided considerable help in such a reassessment, and a business redesign diagram remains prominently displayed in senior managers' offices. While many experienced managers are naturally reluctant to concede a need for external advice and assistance, Lucas Engineering and Systems contribution to the thinking process was recognised and they, in turn, measured their contribution in terms of Pontypool's subsequent improvements as listed above. By January 1988, the reconstruction of the SCS Business was 95 per cent complete, with the disc brake business at 85 per cent and Actuation at 65 per cent completion. A fourth Task Force was set up in late 1987 to consider consumable materials control, and a fifth was set up in mid-1988 to look at the central works

engineering department. Site overhead costs have reduced dramatically by over 50 per cent.

The Lucas "Business - Module - Cell" approach has been generally welcomed by those working within the new structures. Indeed the factory's initial demand that managers at all levels should be more accountable has become a demand from some of those managers that they should be allowed to become even more accountable. They wish to take over more of those functions which remain at factory level, and so operate as closely as possible to the model of an independent "business within a business".

Learning by doing

With hindsight, Pontypool managers concede that mistakes were made which tended to slow down the change process. The Task Force took rather longer than assumed in the Lucas model. This might not have happened if a senior manager had been seconded to work full-time alongside the Task Force, freed from day-to-day demands on his time. There is also sympathy for the view, expressed above, that as many central services as possible should be transferred into the businesses, to make them "as near to completely stand-alone entities as is feasible".

Some other constraining factors were legacies of the pre-CAP days, but were made apparent by the Lucas Engineering and Systems approach. Employee communications was revealed to be particularly ineffective; even allowing for trade union requirements that communication should be through their officials to their members, rather than through managers to employees. Similarly, a skills audit conducted by the Task Force unearthed major problems: "we wanted a flexible workforce, but we didn't realise the depth of skill deficiencies we had to build on". This realisation, together with the communications problem, has given rise to two lessons of wider importance, concerning the Lucas Engineering and Systems approach. As one manager put it: "We only realised late in the day that it was all about training". In future, training in support of these organisational changes "will be planned better, and provided earlier".

Equally, the need to fit cultures to structures
has been recognised. The early emphasis was
heavily upon changing the structures, but less
on policies to develop attitudes in harmony
with those structures. As a result "we had a
brand-new organisation, but the same old
attitudes". That is now changing, not least due
to the review of involvement policies noted
earlier. Social engineering may not be spelled
out in the Lucas Systems Engineering
approach, but it is an essential component of it.
As a result of the successes and experience
gained Lucas Engineering and Systems is now
finding more support for and interest in
'management of change' programmes.

OVERALL MATERIAL FLOW

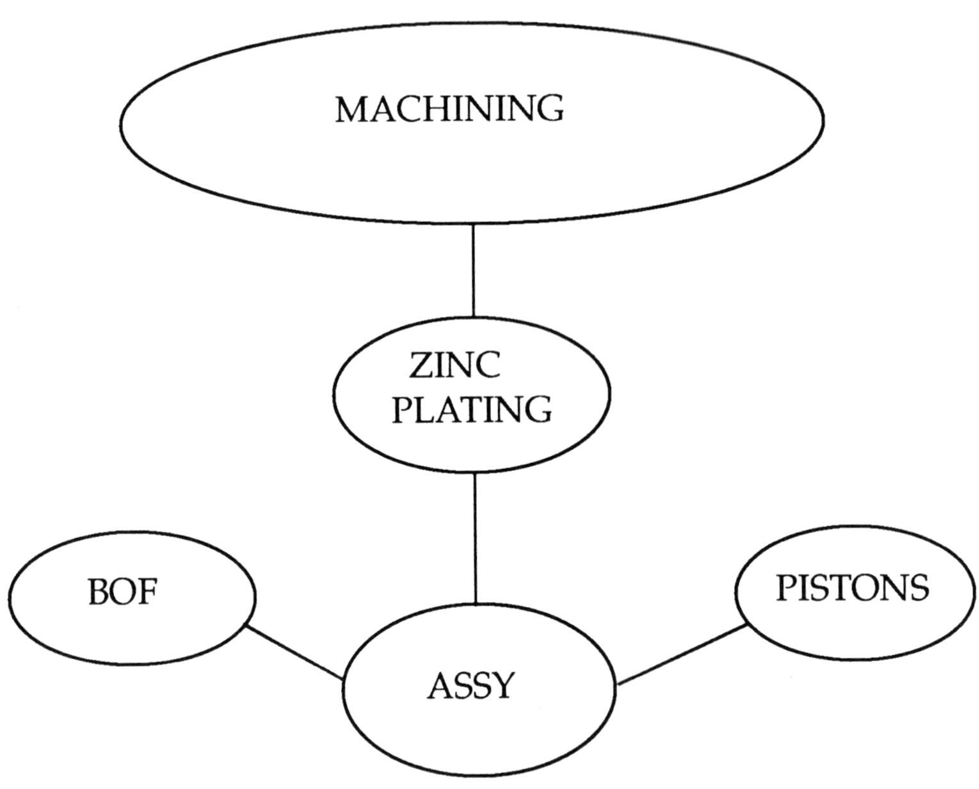

LUCAS CAR BRAKING SYSTEMS, BOUZONVILLE, FRANCE

Girling selected Bouzonville, near Metz, as a site for disc brake production in 1967. It had a number of advantages: location closer to the centre of the European Community; proximity to the Koblenz factory; a reasonably bilingual population because of its closeness to the German border, which would make it easier to learn to operate German machines; an available factory and very important in those early days of labour shortages - a ready supply of labour, both women and ex-miners who were looking for work, (almost 40 per cent of the 1988 labour force were women).

Bouzonville increased output steadily over the first decade. They doubled output between 1970 and 1974, and more than doubled output again by 1979. However, with a recession in the world motor industry, by 1984 output had fallen back by a quarter to 1976 levels.

In many ways the factory typified the Lucas-wide manufacturing problems summarised in the first section. It was set up for volume production of a small range of six products, using mainly special-purpose machinery and unskilled labour. By the 1980s, however, it was trying to produce 96 products, many of them in very small batches. Even investment in expensive, more flexible production machinery was not enabling them to cope.

By 1982/83, most of Bouzonville's performance indicators were looking bad. Output was falling but, relative to output, stocks of materials and work in progress were increasing. With employment stable (just under 1,000), productivity, measured in clocked hours input to standard hours output, was falling. Quality was declining (scrap and work had risen to 3 per cent) and there were major problems meeting delivery dates. The industrial relations climate was hostile, after major strikes in 1978, 1980 and 1981. Absenteeism among the 550 direct workers was 14 per cent, and was 6 per cent for other employees. Annual time lost due to accidents averaged 1 day per employee. This was the situation in which Lucas requested the new general manager to submit a Competitiveness Action Plan for the factory. Given the relative strength and stability of the Koblenz plant, and the existence of other Lucas Girling disc brake facilities in Pontypool and Pamplona, (and, of course, Lucas Girling's two major world-class competitors), Bouzonville's future was in question.

The change process

Producing the CAP made it clear to the general manager that the whole manufacturing process would have to be rethought. Following Lucas practice, he used Lucas Engineering and Systems help in training his senior team in manufacturing systems engineering methodology. They then set up a full-time Task Force. Functions represented on it were accounting, quality control and machining. Trade union members were involved.

The Task Force identified as their priority objective the redesign of the layout of the factory, which was based around a large machine shop. Within the shop, the manufacturing cycle appeared deceptively simple (see Figure 6), involving the machining, zinc plating and then the assembly of the brake castings, piston and a number of bought-out parts. However, the Task Force's analysis of the manufacturing process revealed a picture of great complexity and with key processes having very long changeovers.

There were three key objectives. First, production lead times had to be shortened. Detailed Task Force analysis showed how these were lengthened by a complex "spaghetti" flow of production. Second, stocks of materials and work in progress had to be reduced. It was clear that they were kept high to satisfy the 'output mentality' of the factory, and the requirements of the 'spaghetti-like' production process. Third, over-long changeover times between batches had to be reduced to allow small batch production. These imposed costs arose not only from "down time", but also from machine wear and tear during the changeover process.

Identifying modules

The Task Force decided that the layout had to change. Instead of being based on groups of similar specialist processes and supported by a

FREINS GIRLING TYPICAL PRODUCT LIFE CURVE

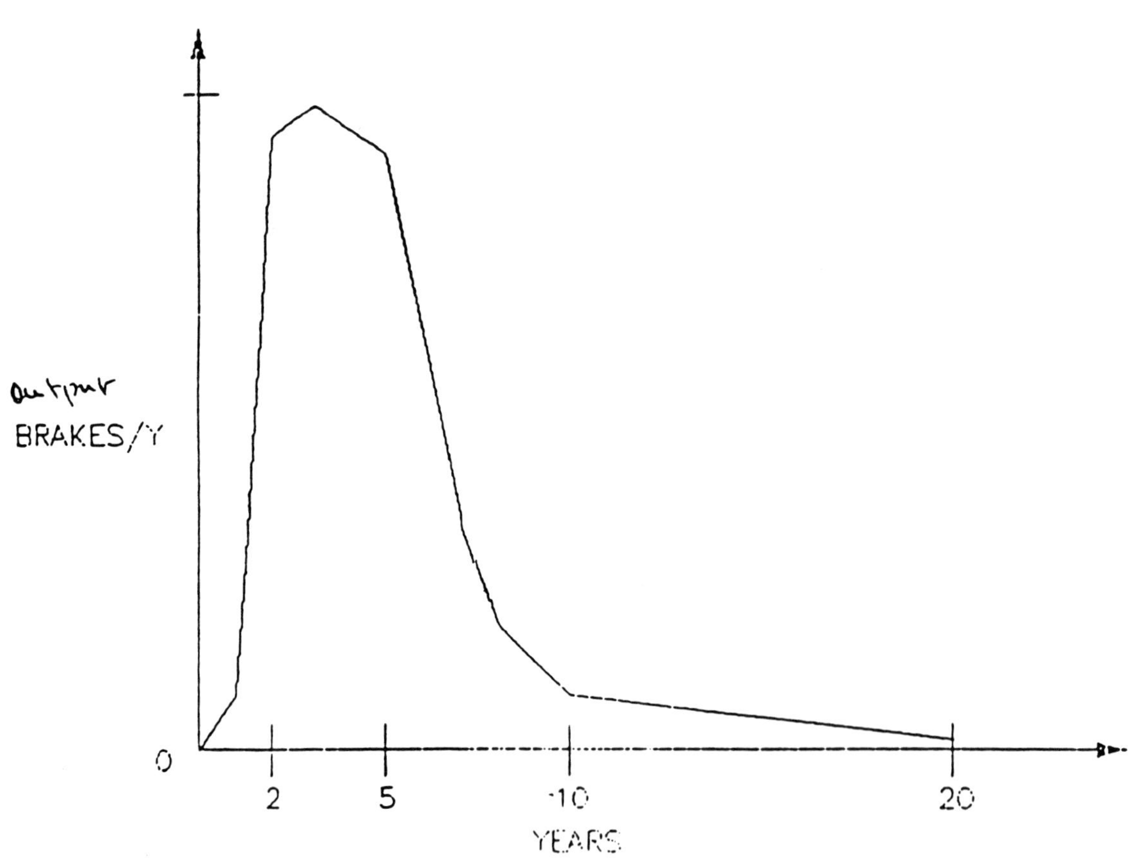

single functionally-based management structure, it was to be based on groups of related products, using a modular structure and cross functional teamworking. But whereas the definition of such product groups had been fairly straightforward at Pontypool (qv) the greater degree of product homogeneity offered Bouzonville's Task Force no 'natural' candidates.

They therefore decided to assess whether modularisation might be based on product life cycles. There was a fund of conventional wisdom about the nature of the factory's product life cycles - much of it subsequently proved wrong - but little hard information. The Task Force therefore collected data on all recent products so as to produce life cycle curves. While different products exhibited different peak volumes, their overall shape was found to be constant.

The separate curves were composited into a single "typical" curve (Figure 7) which showed five distinct phases: pre-production; introduction; full production; falling production; and service. The Task Force recognised that each phase called for a different type of manufacturing system, in terms of both machinery and manpower. The process of analysis therefore offered a basis for modularising the organisation and changing its physical layout appropriately.

The analytical process has been described in some detail because it iillustrates what can be achieved by thorough (and ingenious) application of the Lucas Engineering and Systems analytical approach, based on carefully gathered information, carried out by a most capable multi-functional Task Force, actively directed by a strong manager. As the general manager put it "the analytical planning stage is critical. Therefore it requires top management involvement, leading from the front. The important thing is to choose a Task Force made up not only of people from several disciplines, but of the most capable people. Then give them time to do the job properly".

Top management had to put its full weight behind the implementation process. In this case, the division of production into the four new modules meant the relocation of all but six

of 120 machines. There had also to be no interruption to production for markets which were recovering strongly from the recession. That involved initially making space to enable the relocation into modules to begin.

Eventually, each of the four product-unit modules occupied a distinct area within the factory, with the toolroom in the centre. To ensure employee involvement, the two larger modules were broken down into cells with a maximum of 20 people. The 'spaghetti' was unravelled, and re-formed into seven lines of machines within Red Module, and eight within Yellow.

It all took a long time. The analysis alone consumed five man-years of high-level time (including that of the manufacturing systems engineer). Training the people, restructuring and moving the machines into place took three years. The general manager's view was that because the product design was relatively long lasting, speed of change was not the first priority, a more gradual approach to change could be adopted: "Progres par petits pas"

The four modules were defined as follows and in Figure 8.

High volume (now known as the 'Red Module')

This module would deal with the traditional high volume/low product variety of manufacturing, based on stable designs for known markets. Volumes would be high enough to justify dedicated transfer machines with short change-over time, in classic series or line production, with low stock levels supported by Kanban. In classic Pareto tradition, 20 per cent of products accounted for almost 80 per cent of output.

In manpower terms there could be an easy transition from traditional approaches, since operator skills would be relatively low and a management structure based along functional lines would be effective, so long as the manager was competent in managing people.

LUCAS FIGURE 8:

	HIGH VOLUME	MEDIUM VOLUME	NEW PRODUCTS	SERVICE & PROTOTYPE
Number of types	16	22	typically 2	Over 50
Typical Batch Size Delivery Frequency	- Daily	1000 Weekly	1000 Weekly	100 Monthly to Annual
Machine Types	Large Rotary Transfer Special purpose m/cs	Small Rotary Transfer Multi Spindle CNC	Single Spindle CNC Twin Spindle CNC	Single Spindle CNC Simple Manual m/cs
Product Design	Very Stable	Stable	Frequent Changes	Changes On Request
Fixturing	Classic, Dedicated	Relatively Flexible	Simple, Flexible	Existing or Simple
Production Scheduling	Kanban	Template with Accumulated Kanban	Informal Scheduled	Informal Scheduled
Operator Skill Levels	Low	Low to Average	Medium	High
Module Leader Skills	Human Resource Management	Planning, Scheduling Resource Management	Technical	Technical, Detailed knowledge of old products

Medium volume ('Yellow Module')

In this module, the families of product designs would be stable, but volumes would be insufficient to justify dedicated transfer machines. It would call for small batch production, with the critical activity being frequent change of machine use (a mixture of conventional and CNC machinery) from one product to another.

Operator skills would be higher and broader, and a team module management approach would be needed. As Figure 8 suggests, the manager's critical skill needs would be in planning and levelled scheduling, to minimise costly changeovers.

New products ('Green Module')

With new products coming onto the market more frequently, customers could want the plant to respond urgently to higher demand. Nobody knew whether new products could eventually give rise to high volumes (and hence 'Red Module' dedicated machinery production) because, for instance, the vehiclefor which it was intended might not be a success.

But new products would be the factory's future, so it would need to be able to respond quickly. It was decided to use CNC machines with flexible fixturing for new products, rather than take the risk of laying down tooling for high volume production which might not materialise. That decision had to be postponed as long as possible. However, it was envisaged that those products which did succeed would eventually be relocated on appropriate machines within the Red or Yellow modules.

The management skills required to run such a flexible "machine shop" within a "machine shop" were seen to be different and the importance of technical skills in production was recognised.

After-market spares, service and prototype ('Black Module')

This would be a mixed module in terms of products but with almost identical equipment and manpower inputs to that of the 'Green Module'. Spare service parts for obsolete products were those ending a long life, and were thus to be batch-produced in volumes which would no longer justify the use of high-volume, dedicated machines. The prototypes were obviously at the beginning of what might well be a very short life. Any single prototype was unlikely to be repeated, though a similar design could used in some future prototype.

This module would need to be equipped with flexible, low output CNC machines. Skills would be of the highest order, given the over-riding need to manufacture quickly, with little prepared tooling, and to drawings which would not adequately define the machining route to be used. There would need to be very close links to the technical function when prototyping.

Managing the organisational change

Once the new modular structure was agreed, decisions had to be taken about the relationship between the modules and central services, about appointments (and training those appointed), about consulting the workforce and trade union representatives, and about drawing up training plans for all staff whose jobs would be affected by the restructuring.

The extent of delegation from the centre was much less than at Pontypool (qv). There, a tier of semi-autonomous business managers was interposed between the general manager and the modules; in Bouzonville, with its simpler product structure, this was not thought necessary. The roles of module leaders and cell leaders would, however, be essentially the same as those of Pontypool's module leaders and unit controllers.

Recruitment and training

Five module leaders and (to cover shift working) eighteen cell leaders were appointed. The new module leaders selected were the old section foremen. They were chosen because they were the most experienced candidates and, in a tightly-knit rural community, the social costs of a demotion would not be acceptable. Nevertheless, they required a great deal of training for their new roles, and one appointee subsequently failed to make the grade. The cell leaders came from the ranks of former charge-hands and setters. Theirs was a more considerable step into management, demanding a big development effort. As the general manager noted: "this is where the training burden is greatest".

Training of the new managers in understanding the manufacturing systems approach followed the standard Lucas approach. The general manager had already been trained in the senior management initiative, described in the Lucas section of this report. He assisted the Lucas Engineering and Systems representative to train the management team and the Task Force team. The latter trained the module leaders, then helped them to train their cell leaders, who ultimately trained other employees, many of whose jobs became markedly different.

Consultation

But before training of the workforce as a whole could begin, people had to be prepared for the changes to come and the trade unions had, by law, to be consulted. Then the plans had to be communicated to all employees, especially to the operators who made up half of the labour force. Simply to have given lectures on the 'modular' principles would not have gained support. It was decided to make one production line operative (J48), and then to gain trade union support for the change process on the practical basis of "how it worked".

The management team decided that a series of two-hour workshops should be held, to communicate the nature of, and reasons for, the changes to all employees. The workshops would begin with Cell 1 (one of two cells which would make up 'Red Module') and then be repeated for each new Cell as the reorganisation progressed.

First there was a statutory obligation to inform the works council. When they were first told about it in 1984, many council members interpreted what was being proposed as no more than a technical project. Its real significance only emerged with the appointment of the module leaders and cell leaders. They were clearly being selected for their competence and experience. The trade union members subse-quently saw the change as being "not just about rearranging the machinery, but about giving people more responsibility, and about reinforcing the change in the plant's management style, from instructing to participating".

The unions had been trying to establish better relationships with management since the strike of 1981, which they subsequently recognised as a minor local disaster; it had caused 250 new jobs to go to Koblenz instead of Bouzonville. They were therefore in favour of any initiative "which would create a better environment, in which people would be asked to stretch themselves and be trained to do it". The unions therefore supported the initiative, approved the associated training plan (see below), and offered to help the Task Force to make a slide-tape presentation for the communications workshops. They encouraged their members to accept the changes.

Workshop meetings

The workshops began with a 15-minute presentation and this was followed by questions addressed to Task Force and Works Council members. The presentation showed how the new module/cell structure was a solution to the"spaghetti" process problem, and how the life cycle analysis had led to that solution. It then demonstrated how Cell 1 would work and what effect the reorganisation of production would have on the work of each person on the line.

Many of the effects on the job content of operators were fairly radical. Instead of working at a single machine, operators might operate several different types of machine. Instead of leaving end-inspection to deal with quality, they would have to take more responsibility for inspecting their own work. They would need to make more of a contribution to simple preventive maintenance, and to learn to work in teams.

The whole reorganisation was to be introduced concurrently with a major drive for improved quality. Achieving greater:

• responsabilite - taking more responsibility for the product;

LUCAS FIGURE 9:

EXTRACTS FROM TRAINING PLAN FOR MODULAR WORKING

THEME	SUBJECT	DAYS*
1	Understanding The System - calculating needs, the stocks question, the assembly programme	
2	Alternative Organisation Models - Kanban, Materials Resource Resources, principles of production	10
3	New Administration Needs - redefinition of documentation and procedures	10
4	Module Working - problem solving techniques, basic financial information, value analysis	10
5	Towards "Total Quality" - product knowledge, maintenance techniques, communications	1
6	Organisation Structures - organigram, 'customer' relationships, how modules fit in	
7	Manpower Resourcing - manpower analysis, selection processes, needs identification	7
8	Personnel - group working, participation	5
9	Communications - techniques, 2-way flows	5
10	Training for Trainers - approaches, aids, on-the-job training	5

for the 25 Module Leaders and Cell Leaders only

• conformite - working to plan, and to standard;

• proprete - maintaining a clean, safe work environment;

• equipe - working as a team.

Responses from the workshop meetings were usually positive. There was wide acceptance of the new layout and structures and readiness to accept responsibility, "if it means a change from the old way, of standing at one machine for 8 hours a day". Some operators had reservations about monitoring their own quality, their ability to do preventive maintenance, and whether they could cope with the training. But as a trade union representative told them, "nobody's got to go to university to learn this. We will help you". However, it was recognised that, maybe 3 per cent of the workforce would not be able to cope with the change. They were found suitable work elsewhere in the factory.

As the following summaries of discussions in the (high-volume) Red Module show, the new system brought significant changes to the work of module leaders, cell leaders and setters as well as operators. In general, while these have been welcomed, putting the system into practice has not been without difficulties.

Changing responsibilities

The Module Leaders' job has been made much more demanding than the former Section Foremen's role. (The modular structures in Girling have allowed young graduates to be given broad experience as module leaders early in their careers). They are now fully responsible for all aspects of production of a range of products, from start to finish, instead of for a bank of machines. As the general manager put it when making the appointments: "you are going to be a general manager and I will buy your output". The role imposes quite new responsibilities, such as investment planning, production planning, and decisions about material control (ie whether to introduce a Kanban system). It also involves managing twice as many people, 155 compared to 80, though in practice much of this is devolved to cell leaders. The 'human management' issues take considerable time, particularly in building

team work among operatives. Overall, the job is "more difficult, and more interesting".

The cell leaders' task has also become markedly different from their previous foreman duties. They are now responsible for work done on a wider range of machines (as against a single type), making fewer products (as against all 96 products), and for the complete product and material flow (as against a single machining operation). The new system is seen to be far superior in that it offers: "involvement in the whole process, more authority to organise it, and more freedom to decide how to organise it".

Finally, the setter was just a setter under the old system, responsible only for the setting of 30 drilling machines. (Management anticipated difficulties at this level, because some of the setters had highly-specialised skills). A setter interviewed during the case study was responsible for setting five machines, of different types. But the job had changed to include a wide range of new activities which would previously have been done by other specialists, for example:

- controlling material flows and moving people around (management tasks);

- doing analyses of machine "down time" the foreman did that;

- intervening in the machining programme (normally a technician's task);

- suggesting modifications which would increase output and improve safety (like an engineer).

In total, the job had become "more interesting, with more responsibility. But the point was, we just had to change something in the organisation, to try to improve prospects".

Providing the enabling policies

The changes outlined demanded a major training effort. Simply to cope with the effects of reorganisation, a 3-day workshop of Task Force members, Module Leaders and a training consultancy formulated a 10-part programme, are outlined in Figure 9.

Some elements of the 56 day training programme (not all of which has yet been
completed) also applied to groups of staff other
than the new, critically-important, module
leaders and cell leaders. Bouzonville's 3-year,
115-page training plan analyses in great detail
the training needs for all occupational groups.
The total provision is:

36,090 hours (1987)
44,435 hours (1988)
27,240 hours (1989)

The 1988 provision averaged 43 hours per
employee, about 2 per cent of contracted
working time. The trade unions pointed out
that the figure was five times the statutory
minimum. Even so, nobody pretends it is
enough. Interviewees at most levels would
welcome more training, preferably with a
switch of emphasis away from technical training and towards management development,
personnel management and communications
techniques, because "you can't just expect
suddenly to become one big family".

Several case studies in this series, and including
the Pontypool study, refer to the way in which
other personnel policies have been adjusted in
order to assist the change management process
in general, and the organisation of work tasks
in particular. Bouzonville has carried through
its quite significant re-organisation with
remarkably few adjustments other than the
training programme and the associated
communications events.

It seems there was little need for other changes.
Consultative arrangements are established by
law, through the Works Council and through
'droit d'expression' group discussions. There
was no need to negotiate a flexible working
agreement, since most people were already
prepared to work flexibly within their
competence and the job's requirements. No
employment guarantees were given, (though
the changes involved no job loss). The trade
unions did not seek higher pay for their
members' extra 'responsibilite'; in their view the
reorganisation promised more important
rewards in terms of "more secure employment
for the future, more worthwhile jobs today, and
a working environment in which management
listens to people". This is not to say that all

these arrangements worked perfectly in
support of the change. One feeling was that the
single rate of pay for operatives should be
supplemented by some payment-by-results
element. Some shop floor employees wanted
more information about new models, the order
book and the future production programme.

The statutory provisions on involvement, and
especially the droit d'expression, are thought by
some (including the managers) to be
inadequate; the feedback has been very limited
so far. But the general view is that a lot of
progress has been made and (to quote a Works
Council member): "If only we can get these
policies right, we will wipe the floor with the
competition".

How much progress?

On any type of measure, the improvement has
been considerable. Even with only a slightly
higher output volume, (just over 4 million
brakes a year), over 4 years the value of sales
increased by 60 per cent; pre-tax profit went up
by 1,000 per cent. The all-important ratio of
work in progress to output fell by 55 per cent
while labour productivity had risen by 12 per
cent; both of these indicators owe much to the
reorganisation. Quality (measured by the level
of scrap and rework) has risen by up to 45 per
cent, much of it as a result of operators check-
ing their own quality.

The plant achieved the ability to deliver on a
daily basis, through its improved capability to
meet production schedules. In the manpower
area, the number of accidents halved and
absenteeism fell by 25 per cent but is still
thought to be too high. Most managers felt that
these improvements reflected a growing "sense
of purpose" about the organisation which could
be tracedback to the increasingly participative
style of management.

However, participative style proved less easy to
put in place than the 120 new machines.
Managers at all levels lost their former power
and control in the changed environment. Some
did not change their attitudes significantly; as
one interviewee said "changing from 'screw' to
colleague is not easy". Even for the most committed managers, getting to grips with the
human relations dimension of their new jobs

was taking time. And the familiar divide between shop floor and central departments - "we are trying to introduce team working; but are they?" - had been found present to some degree. But even these exceptions served to highlight the major improvement in atmosphere which had already been wrought.

Senior managers recognised some aspects of the change process which (with hindsight) might have been handled differently, and will be built into future initiatives. In future, they said, the rank and file would be taken into the process earlier and much more detailed information would be made available. Future Task Forces would increasingly need specialist personnel involvement, because the barriers to change had (as Lucas said) 70 per cent to do with methodology and hence with changing people's attitudes. The same planned "first, make space" approach which was applied to re-siting the machines would be applied to reorganising the manpower.

The Lucas contribution

Bouzonville's top management enthusiastically supports the Lucas approach to managing change. The requirement to produce a viable CAP was seen as "a necessary shock to the system. Without it, we would not have been in business". The manufacturing systems engineering methodology for thinking through the change process is seen as helpful, as is the Task Force mechanism for leading that process. A Task Force will next be set up to make recommendations on automating the assembly process. The factory manager's view was that, for maximum effectiveness, Task Forces should be "one at a time; staffed with the best people; and a good team should be kept together for the next job". The availability of a Lucas Engineering and Systems resource was thought to be important, not least because it provided a form of 'internal' consultancy, which keeps knowledge within the business and keeps fully up to date with best world practice. (Bouzonville made it fully internal, by recruiting the Lucas Engineering and Systems consultant at the end of the project.

On change management more generally, Bouzonville's top management felt that a number of guiding principles, most of them inherent in the Lucas approach, should be borne in mind, including:

- management should lead from the front, and get involved in detailed aspects of change;

- management style must be consistent with the change objectives; in this case, a "patriarchal" style was most appropriate;

- but management should not assume they know all the answers; they should always consult the people closest to the problem;

- these people ultimately have to own the problem, if it is to be solved, and "people will always tend to rise to the occasion, given the opportunity";

- for continuing change, train, train and train again;

- throughout, develop and maintain excellent human relations.

MB GROUP AND NEATH INDUSTRIAL COMPONENTS

CREATING A CLIMATE FOR CHANGE

Like Lucas, MB Group's roots are in engineering. They suffered a considerable financial setback in the early 1980s and the subsidiary featured in the case study, Neath Industrial Components in South Wales, looked set for eventual closure.

MB Group helped transform its performance by changing the way in which its subsidiaries set and pursued their objectives. The MB Group Chairman asked subsidiaries to "bring me your solutions". The Group has turned from being a centrally-directed organisation to one in which the operating units are empowered to determine their own routes to success.

Within this framework, Neath Industrial Components, a highly unionised plant, with several union bargaining units, has achieved a major shift in management, shop floor and union attitudes. Instead of facing closure Neath now has an expansion and modernisation programme of almost £15million.

Background

MB Group is the name adopted by the former Metal Box at its annual general meeting on 21 July 1988.

The change of name symbolises of the corporate changes which have taken place particularly over the last 3 years, in attitudes and culture as well as organisationally.

Metal Box can trace its origins back more than 200 years. The MB Group now has a turnover of £1.239 billion (1988 figures) and profits before tax of £94.1m. Some 28500 employees are engaged in 23 countries in the four core business areas of the Group: the production of food and beverage packaging, speciality packaging and engineering products, heating and bathroom products, and cheques and business forms. Around 17000 employees are based in the UK, about half of the number employed in the early 1970s.

The MB subsidiary with which this case study is mostly concerned, Neath Industrial Components (NIC), is one of 10 UK packaging business units, which together account for half the total Group turnover.

NIC has a turnover of £62m and employs 557 permanent employees. Some 50 per cent of turnover is accounted for by inter-unit trading within MB. This contrasts with an 80 per cent dependence in the period 1980/81. At that time NIC had a turnover of £52m and employed 2600 people, down from a peak of 3000 in the late 1960s and early 1970s.

NIC is primarily a producer of can components but is also known for its printing and lacquery of tin plate. NIC products are to be seen in everyday use: food and beverage cans, soft drink cans and Stripseal ends for oil cans. NIC's main product is the Easy Open End, or EOE, with its characteristic ring tag for easy opening. NIC makes some 3 billion of these each year.

The need for change

Change at Neath has gone hand in hand with change in MB, with changes in both having common origins in the period 1979/81. Change at Neath, however, can only be understood in the context of the efforts of the Group to set itself on a new course in the early 1980s. This Group change may be divided into two parts, the first of which concerned a process of financial stabilisation, rationalisation and improved performance. The second phase, beginning in the mid 1980s, is more associated with the break-up of the corporate headquarters, devolution and culture change.

In 1979 the MB Group suffered a combination of setbacks for which it was ill-prepared. It had high gearing and borrowings which rose by 1982 to £227 million. The Group was also hit by the effects of technological innovation in the form of the "two piece" can, which effectively halved the output requirements of the Neath plant. Further, the Group's moves into new can-making technology were less effective than those of the competition, which provided a fourth setback by establishing manufacturing facilities within the UK. The result was the loss of market share at a time of domestic as well as international over-capacity.

MB FIGURE 1:

COMPARATIVE STATISTICS 1981 AND 1988

		1981	1988
Sales	- £m	827.0*	1239.0
Profit before tax	- £m	0.8*	84.1
Earnings per share	- Pence	1.9	23.4
Sales/employee	- £	19,600.0	45,600.0
Net borrowings	- £m	145.0	23.0
Gearing (net)	- %	42.0	7.0
Interest cover	times	2.1	8.9
Return on capital	- %	11.4	30.5
Market capitalisation	- £m	138.0	728.0

excluding South Africa and Nigeria

As a response to these problems came the first phase of corporate change, which was directly concerned with ensuring the survival of the Group. At the time the UK operations were just breaking even and a dividend could only be financed from the proceeds from international operations. A new financial director was appointed on 1 December 1981 and subsequently a team of 12 people was brought together to implement a new system of financial management and set the Group on a new financial course.

As can be seen from Figure 1, the financial results have been impressive and have underpinned the second level of changes which began in the mid 80s. Virtually every indicator of financial performance has seen year on year improvement since 1981.

Comparative Statistics 1981 and 1988

The second phase of change

In spite of the considerable improvements in the Group's financial performance (and in all other performance indicators, such as sales per employee) it was recognised that the Group remained very much what it had always been, a centrally directed corporation with all the styles and attitudes typical of that kind of organisation. As it has since been put, "too many problems went to the HQ and never got an answer". Headquarters was staffed by some 600 people, which represented a considerable overhead in staffing costs. It also required considerable management time because of the demands of an extended decision-taking process. It was a problem that had been under consideration for some time. In 1979 McKinsey and Co, the international consulting group, had carried out a study of the case for decentralisation and made recommendations in its favour. However, the task of setting the Group on a new financial course had overshadowed the issue until 1985, by which time the Group was running on a secure financial basis. Also, at that time the Group Chairman was due to retire.

Consequently the second phase of change began with a search for a Chairman who could provide leadership for the programme of decentralisation and devolution, with the implicit aim of reducing the HQ to a small core of supporting, facilitating and enabling staff. The Group was concerned to make an appointment of someone who could contribute to and communicate the new vision of the company which the Group was aiming for.

The appointment of the new Chairman, who joined the Board in April 1985 but didn't formally take up his post until January 1986, represented the culmination of a process of consensus building among senior executives which had been going on since 1981. A 1983 meeting of top executives, held in Oxford, was a particularly important point in this process. This meeting recognised that "the Group had not been punching its weight". The need for a new sense of direction was commonly agreed on.

As a result of this lengthy preparatory period when the new Chairman was appointed (at the time as a director) the Group was able to move with considerable speed. In November 1985 a new organisational approach was announced. It had two key elements. The first made clear that: "the heads of individual (business) units, wherever possible will have direct control over all the resources influencing the short and long term success of their businesses, and will deploy the resources to achieve strategic objectives agreed by the Board". The second element related to the way in which heads of business units would report directly to an executive group consisting of Group Board members, thereby cutting out intervening levels of authority between business units and the board.

Each business unit was required to report to the "Executive Group as a whole" and each member of the Group was required to "assist the heads of businesses". Each Executive group member was to be responsible for overseeing a number of units while also assuming responsibilities for certain functions. These changes were to be carried out within less than two months, and were to be completed "no later than 1 January 1986". The corporate headquarters was to be vacated as soon as possible thereafter. Except for a small core of 130, headquarters personnel were absorbed into the business units.

Change at Neath

Neath's progress from 1979 onward has obviously been greatly influenced during the main change periods within the Group, between 1979 and 1984 and from 1985 to the present.

In Neath's heyday in the late 1960s the MB Group was largely dependent on the plant for can end manufacture. A glittering array of machines were at work, 42 Open Top presses, 9 Aerosol lines, 6 Stripseal units, 14 printlines, 11 lacquer lines, 18 metal scrollers and 7 slitters. Over 3000 people were employed. Such was the plant's prestige that it received the distinction of a visit from Her Majesty the Queen in 1977 but by this time, employment had already passed its peak. Later, in 1984, it received the Queen's Award for Export. Between the two dates employment at Neath had fallen by 60 per cent and by the end of 1984 was down to 983 employees.

A strike at Neath, in the early 1970s had exposed the dependence on it of other Metal Box units. This led to a corporate decision to change the strategy for can end manufacturing and to create alternative manufacturing capabilities in previously Neath-dependent units.

The late 1970s also saw the introduction of the two piece can, mentioned earlier, and this further eroded NIC's position within the Group, raising the question whether or not the plant was really necessary.

In 1979, Metal Box took the strategic decision, in principle, that the Neath operation was no longer required. Subsequently, the plant was separately incorporated as Neath Industrial Components (NIC), with the purpose of progressively detaching it from the other MB UK factories.

The MB Board offered Neath two choices: continue as a supply factory and gradually run down operations - with a life expectancy of 3 to 5 years through loss of business; or reconstruct the business "to a commercially driven operation, seeking its own markets for current products and to diversify into others".

In 1980 the management and unions agreed to the second option, accepting at the same time the substantial reduction of the workforce with the aim of achieving profitable operation by 1983. In essence, NIC became the precursor of the autonomous business units have now been established throughout Metal Box, but without the real autonomy to construct positive business plans that was subsequently granted.

As indicated below, the creation of NIC was intepreted in a number of ways by those employed at Neath and this coloured their attitudes for some time to come:

• the creation of NIC was not a supportive gesture by the MB Board. They were allowing the plant to sink or swim;

• the key task at NIC was the management of inevitable decline. Success in diversifying out of a mature business could defer but not avoid the ultimate result;

• corporate level attitudes towards the plant's future were not favourable;

• pride in years of direct participation in Metal Box was turned into a feeling of second class citizenship;

• some employees worked to see the plant succeed, while many wished to see it fail in order to collect retirement and redundancy pay;

• NIC's hands were tied in making the best use of its most important resource, people, by national level bargaining on conditions and Metal Box divisional bargaining on wages. The result was that NIC's only real control over labour costs was through redundancy;

• the continued round of redundancy programmes was a constant reminder to everyone that the business was slowly bleeding to death;

• each tranche of redundancies destroyed trust between unions and management as each programme was thought to be the last;

• the continuing rundown of the workforce made co-operation between unions more difficult as each sought to safeguard the interests of its own members;

• establishing co-operation between the 10 different bargaining units in the Neath plant became increasingly important to the creation of positive attitudes to change but increasingly more difficult to secure as time went on.

In spite of all its difficulties NIC management attempted to turn the plant around. By 1982, 50 per cent of NIC's output was sold to export markets, though its financial results remained disappointing. In spite of receiving the Queen's Award for Export in 1984, the plant was forced into further redundancies. These caused further problems, as the loss of skills and experience began to be felt. In 1985 there were further redundancies as, in a poor summer for beverage sales, plant orders dropped sharply. This highlighted the difficulty of diversifying out of a high volume/low margin business. A further 287 redundancies were made in April 1986 and another 130 in September 1986. In all, the redundancy and retirement programme had cost the company £13 million. Throughout the period NIC did all it could to improve the core business. Almost 300 working practice changes were made in 1981 alone. An attempt was made to retain skills wherever possible. Non-skilled temporary employees were taken on to act as a redundancy buffer in the event of further redundancy programmes. The management structure was reduced and flattened. Costs were reduced wherever possible and stricter financial accounting was applied. Nevertheless, by September 1985 losses were in excess of £2 million and seemed to point to an inevitable conclusion. At this point however, the Metal Box had already embarked on its new programme of change.

Attitudinal change

To say that Metal Box had not been deeply concerned with the fate of NIC would be to create the wrong impression. The plant was under continuing scrutiny at group level. A detailed review was carried out in 1983 as part of the strategic planning process. Other reviews followed. The view was that if Neath could move successfully into lower volume/ higher margin business aiming at specialised markets then it might have a viable future. Nevertheless, decisions on NIC's future were evolved through a number of corporate layers.

The process was lengthy and created uncertainty. Consequently, the break-up of corporate headquarters in late 1985 marked not only a major organisational change but induced a shift in attitudes. The responsibility for Neath was now seen by NIC's management as being much more in their hands.

The Board positively encouraged its units, through a number of statements and visits, to come up with proposals for growth and expansion and made it clear that it wanted ideas in which it could invest. NIC management was able therefore to stop managing on the basis of "if you don't do this we'll have to close", to one of "if we do this then we can be successful". A further important change, it was said, was that in the past the centre kept solving our problems. Now they were saying, "bring me your solutions".

As far as financial results are concerned the new values can be seen to be working. NIC was nursed through a period of further redundancies in April and September 1986. In both 1986 and 1987 it met its Business Plan, and in 1988 saw a modest profit for the first time in many years. Optimism is visibly growing with the installation of a new £1.6m line for EOEs. More importantly, in 1988 a £14.5m investment programme for the modernisation of the plant had been put on the table (this includes £4.8m funding from the Welsh Office). It is the most significant manifestation, but not the only one, of the "bring me your solutions" philosophy. The Board is no longer seen as a controlling power, more as an enabling force. The attitudinal shift within NIC is considerable, though many problems remain. At this early stage in the process of change it is interesting to look at the way in which problems are being tackled.

Industrial relations and the personnel function. The collective bargaining arrangements at NIC are outlined above. It is not surprising that industrial relations difficulties arose, given the situation which faced the plant. Until 1986, national level bargaining took place in four different forums while some bargaining was devolved only to divisional level. At plant level ten different bargaining units were (and still are) involved, including two involving one union. Management at all levels in MB and the unions, both at national and local level, have been working hard to rationalise the structure and to decentralise responsibility for these matters.

Since 1986, national level bargaining has been devolved to divisional level and enabling agreements have been sought to bring about full local bargaining on a multi-union basis. NIC has secured a degree of local bargaining as a result of the 1985-86 difficulties, but there is still someway to go.

The fact that MB has made it clear that taking responsibility also means taking responsibility for local bargaining has been, at Neath, a very important signal to everyone there that their future is very much in their own hands. Commitment to succeed at all levels in the plant has, as a result, received an important boost. As was said, "When you are trying to create a greenfield environment in a brown field site, you need a lot of commitment".

Communications, leadership and trust. The fall and rise of Neath has been reflected in the pattern of communications. A factory council was started around 1980, but without the support of all the unions. "It fell apart by 1984". Team briefings were attempted in 1983 but lasted only a year. Management communication with the shop floor throughout this period was essentially through the shop steward system. In the main, the only news was bad news.

Since 1985/86, a new impetus has been given to improving communications. Again, the 'role modelling' from the centre has been an important factor in creating credibility for a new approach. The MB Executive Group are seen to get out to the plants and talk with people at all levels. Such visits have been seen as a continuous process of top level interest in and support for what is going on at plant level. Early in 1988 the Board reinforced its communication policies in a comprehensive statement called "Creating a Climate for Change". This states that, "there will be a corporate level (communications) programme driven by the chairman and executive group".

Within the Group the aims of the programme are to:

• restate the commitment of Metal Box to be an excellent company;

• explain why it is important for Metal Box to gain and keep competitive edge;

• describe the sorts of behaviour appropriate to success;

• provide support, recognition and public acknowledgement of employees;

• motivate employees to give their best because they are proud to work for MB Group.

It is within this supportive climate from the centre that NIC has been able to begin the long process of creating a new environment, and rebuild communications. A joint consultation group for the plant is being established. Briefing meetings began again in 1986. In this process of reconstruction, NIC's management and unions have recognised the importance of building trust. "Whenever management and unions came together in the past it was to discuss redundancies".

Equally important has been the creation of a cohesive and effective management team. This has been tackled by off site meetings of management to discuss strategy and also through schemes in which management team members evaluate each others' strengths and weaknesses. This programme has been coupled with team role laboratories, for managers, to develop candour and team contributions. "We are striving for consensus so that we can move forward as a team. It is the only way to create confidence".

Training. In a period when employment at NIC has fallen by 85 per cent in less than a decade, it may be surprising that any training has taken place. Neath, in fact, had a proud tradition of training. In the late 1940s it opened an apprentice training centre. In 1954 it opened a production training centre. In the 1980s, almost inevitably with so many redundancies, training activities were curtailed but never

stopped. The numbers of apprentices taken on
fell as the redundancy programme gathered
pace. The company still continues to take on
apprentices: four were taken on in 1988, two for
mechanical engineering and two for printing.
The production training centre still remains,
although reduced to a one man operation.

A number of factors have led to the retention of
the training effort. The 1985/86 redundancy
programme was carried through with the aim
of retaining the skill base of the plant. At a time
when electronic control systems were becoming
more important, training in these technologies
was essential. Nevertheless, Neath is now
suffering from skill shortages in specialist areas.
For the future Neath is proposing to move to a
skill related pay system - based on a comprehensive skills development programme. Flexibility and training are seen to be interdepend-
ent. The fact that such matters are being
negotiated is a measure of the change of climate
which has taken place at Neath.

The future

The visitor to Neath is struck by the range of
changes going on: plant modernisation,
investment programmes, industrial relations
restructuring, new pay and training proposals,
diversification into new products, expansion of
the sales force and a search for new markets
and general rationalisation. Each calls for
considerable time and effort. All of these
activities owe a considerable amount to MB's
newly created policy framework and the
positive attitudes which have resulted.

MB for its part has been steadily reinforcing
this framework in important ways. These
include: management succession and resourcing planning; an executive incentive scheme;
and a programme to accelerate the pace of
change.

Management Succession and Resource
Planning. The Group carried out a major
review of management succession and
resource in December 1986. Its aim was to
ensure that the necessary resources and management skills would be available to meet the
long term business resources and objectives of
the Group. The review, which was updated in

March 1988, identified priorities for action. It
also provided a planning framework for matching business opportunities with individual
development needs.

The March 1988 review examined progress
under 37 headings, including training for
'strategic thinking', 'innovation objectives', 'self-
development policy improvement' and 'cross-
business project teams'.

The review concluded that it would continue to
be necessary to regularly review the Group's
needs as the Group matured and changed.

Executive incentive scheme. The Group has
been concerned to relate its executive reward
system to performance. It introduced a new
scheme for the financial year ending 31 March
1988. The scheme identified three categories of
eligible participants, namely, main board
directors, divisional directors and similar job
evaluated posts and other management grades
below this level, including factory managers.

The scheme recognises the need for linkages
between the performance of directors, group
and divisional staff and factory managers, and
the setting of their personal performance
targets. In this sense, the scheme provides an
incentive framework that bonds the organisation together. At main board level performance
is measured on the basis of earnings per share
and individual goals. At factory manager level
the basis of measurement includes earnings per
share and targets set for the business unit and
individual managers. In this way personal
objectives are related to the wider company
interest and the objectives of each level of
operations are related to that of other levels.

Accelerating the pace of change. In January
1988 the Group produced a paper entitled
'Creating a Climate for Change'. This
reiterated the Group's goal of achieving
"worldwide leadership in our chosen fields by
an emphasis on customer needs, technical
excellence and manufacturing performance".
One of the many important features of the
paper was a proposal for a "campaign across
Metal Box for a broad programme of change,
rather than (the tackling of) each change objective as a separate initiative".

METAL BOX GROUP - AGENDA FOR CHANGE

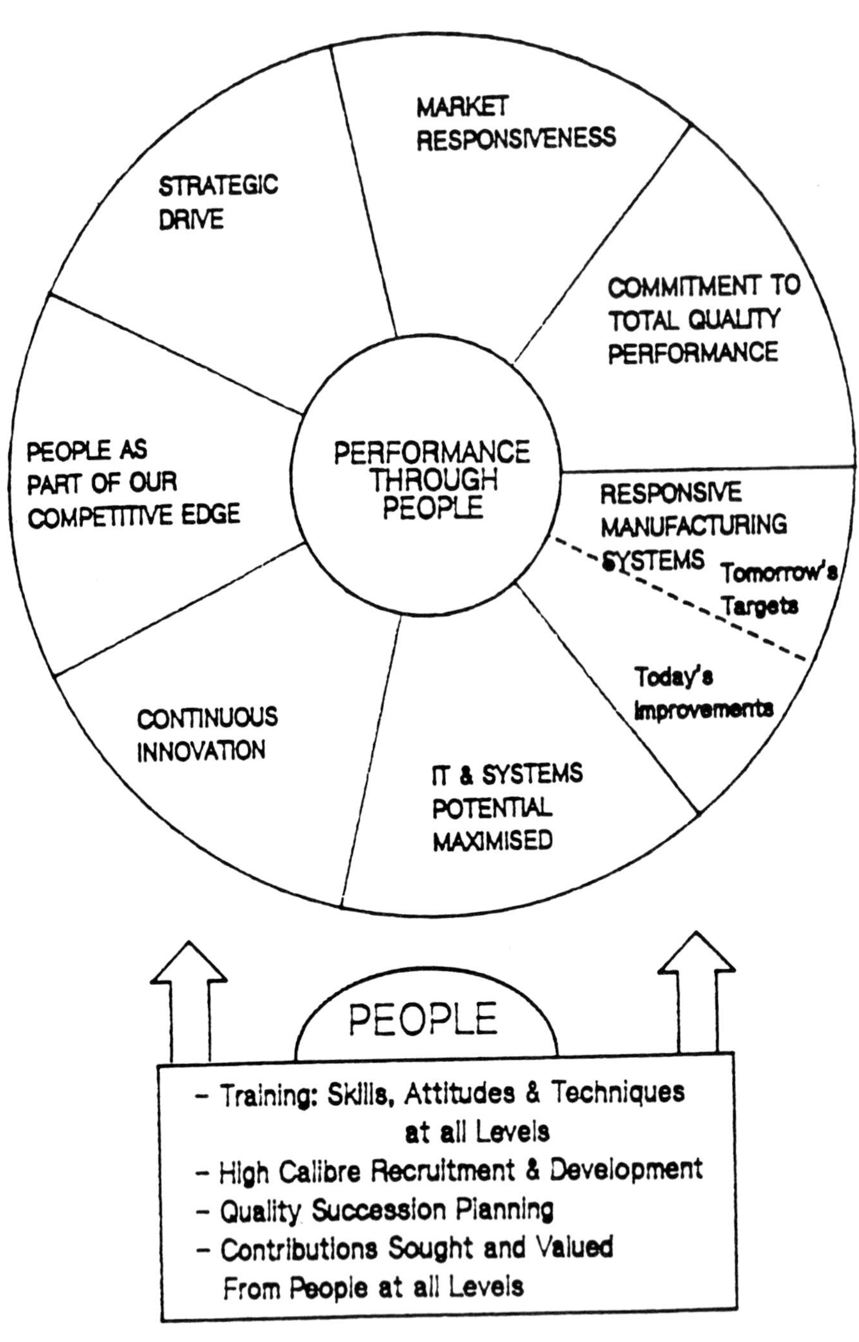

The paper set an Agenda for Change (see Figure 2) which placed improved performance, through people, at the heart of the exercise. The paper acted as a catalyst for debate and consultation on organisational behaviour throughout the Group. Among the desired features of organisations identified in the paper were the following:

• managers will see people as our strength and not our problem;

• training will be an investment and not a cost;

• self development will be actively encouraged;

• innovative and risk-taking achievement will be recognised and rewarded;

• ideas for change and improvements will flow naturally from people at all levels.

Signals sent out to the operating units with the intention of encouraging the adoption of new attitudes have been regular and consistent. They have also been of increasing clarity and commitment as the change programme has progressed. It is not surprising therefore that at NIC attitudes have successfully swung from negative to positive and management there believes it has a mandate to "grow the business". The Group now wants to build on this positive attitudinal shift, at NIC and elsewhere.

The Action for Change programme was fundamentally different from the Group's earlier efforts to bring about change. It was intended to encourage the creation of organisational behaviour capable of continuous change: "the generation of a widespread attitude among all employees that encourages change and innovation". It is intended that the programme will be reinforced through communication and training initiatives.

The MB change programme has been directly concerned with changing attitudes within the operational units and the generation of local commitment to drive up the level of local initiative. NIC believe these policies have been successful. Though many serious problems remain to be resolved, NIC now believes it has a mandate "to grow the business", as well as the attitude of mind needed to make that a reality.

PRATT & WHITNEY

THE SEARCH FOR COMPETITIVE ADVANTAGE

For two reasons this is an interesting example of a move into computer-integrated manufacturing. First, the productivity and quality goals of the plant represent a major step forward from the company's previous performance level. Second, the employment policies, developed to meet specific requirements of the plant, represent a significant change from those used in other Pratt & Whitney plants.

The case-study shows that the plant's success depends as much on the human resource principles which have been applied as on the application of advanced technology. The case-study suggests that this kind of 'factory of the future' will rely on the predominance of technically qualified college personnel to ensure its effectiveness.

Background

Pratt & Whitney (P&W) is the world's biggest manufacturer of jet engines for aircraft. It is the largest unit within United Technologies Corporation (UTC), the world's 38th largest company. P&W has sales of $5.5 billion and employs 47,000 people, with headquarters in Hartford, Connecticut, USA, where it runs its main plant covering some five million square feet.

This case study concerns the setting up of P&W Canada's Halifax, Nova Scotia greenfield plant which was formally opened on 5 November 1987. The plant represents both UTC's and Pratt & Whitney's search for new levels of productivity, quality, customer satisfaction and employee commitment.

The Nova Scotia plant supplies machined parts for P&W's jet engines but was conceived as a plant which could achieve the even higher standards of technical sophistication and reliability required of parts to be used in 'tomorrow's passenger and military aircraft markets. These objectives were thought to be attainable only by making the Halifax plant a computer-integrated manufacturing facility

using the most sophisticated equipment and working practices.

The application of very advanced technology was thought to be a necessity if the company was to obtain the highest quality standards and performance improvements. It was also thought that it would be necessary to match the use of advanced technology with a new approach to working practices. It was thought that the creation of what P&W called a balanced 'socio-technical working environment' would be essential. This case study describes the creation of P&W's 'socio-technical system' or STS as they refer to it.

Reasons for change

Since the early 1980s there had been a growing consciousness in UTC and in P&W that the underlying performance of the Corporation and its divisions needed to be raised to new levels if the company was to continue to succeed in the 21st century.

At the same time, both UTC and P&W became increasingly aware that significant additional productivity gains could not be made by simply introducing new equipment into traditional working environments. As one P&W executive said, "throwing technology at your problems simply doesn't work any more". The working environment and relationships in new plants had themselves to be changed if the capabilities of technology were to be fully realised.

Established working practices were known to have too many interfaces and managing them was found to consume a good deal of management energy, detracting attention from improving the underlying performance rate. The old environment was characterised by little trust in people and particularly by the fact that "only 10 per cent of the workforce was required to do any thinking". Generally, the potential for developing 'cognitive skills' was seen to be unused and undeveloped. In contrast, the Japanese were known to place emphasis on using all their peoples' capabilities. P&W's traditional work environment was considered incapable of accommodating the Japanese approach. P&W set out its perception of the traditional work environment as follows:

- specialised people;

- witheld information;

- autocratic;

- money motivated;

- no risk taking;

- competition between employees.

All these factors were thought to be incompatible with the productivity goals which had to be achieved "if P&W were to survive". They were also seen to be completely at odds with the crucial task of securing a competitive return on the high capital cost of a new high tech plant, such as Halifax.

The change objective - the social system

The targets, in basic productivity terms for the Halifax plant, were:

- to reduce deviations from specification to 1 per cent of the level achieved in a conventional P&W plant;

- to reduce product cycle time by 80 per cent of current practice.

These formidable quality and output objectives were to require considerable financial investment in a computer-integrated manufacturing system. The software costs alone amounted to $20 million (Canadian) for a system which involved 2 million lines of machine code and 100,000 man hours to programme. It took 1000 man hours to programme the machining of one particular part.

To make the 'people' aspects of running the plant compatible with the plant's technological capabilities, P&W have created what they call their 'STS' or 'socio-technical system'. This required the systematic reversal of traditional employment practices, the encouragement of new employee attitudes and new approaches to work.

It was agreed that in place of employee competition there would be collaboration. Functional specialisation would be replaced with flexibility. Allowing employees to do no more than was asked of them needed to be replaced by a willingness on their part to take risks and solve problems spontaneously; downtime in a high technology plant would be too costly to "wait on procedures". Openness would be required in place of protection of information; people would need to use their initiative rather than await orders. In essence, the creation of participation and commitment "to the work and not to the pay cheque" were seen to be key targets in the new approach which would affect work group and other, interpersonal, relationships.

The change process: start-up

Managing the creation of a high-tech plant and the simultaneous introduction of new, and for P&W revolutionary, work practices was recognised as a formidable task requiring technical and human resource skills of a very high order from the person overseeing the process. Although they would normally look within the company for a chief executive, P&W gave an outsider this responsibility. The decision to appoint an outsider was taken in order to avoid the transferring of P&W's established cultural habits to the new plant at the outset.

The Halifax plant manager was appointed in the first instance as deputy to a P&W project manager, a position held for eight months. This period afforded a period of acclimatisation and project familiarisation. The period also provided P&W with an opportunity to evaluate their appointee, who became plant manager and the first employee of the Halifax plant in September 1985.

The calendar of events there after was as follows:

- appointment of change consultants - October 1985

- Search Conference' - November 1985

- confirmation of plant manager - April 1986

PRATT & WHITNEY FIGURE 1:

THE HALIFAX ORGANISATION

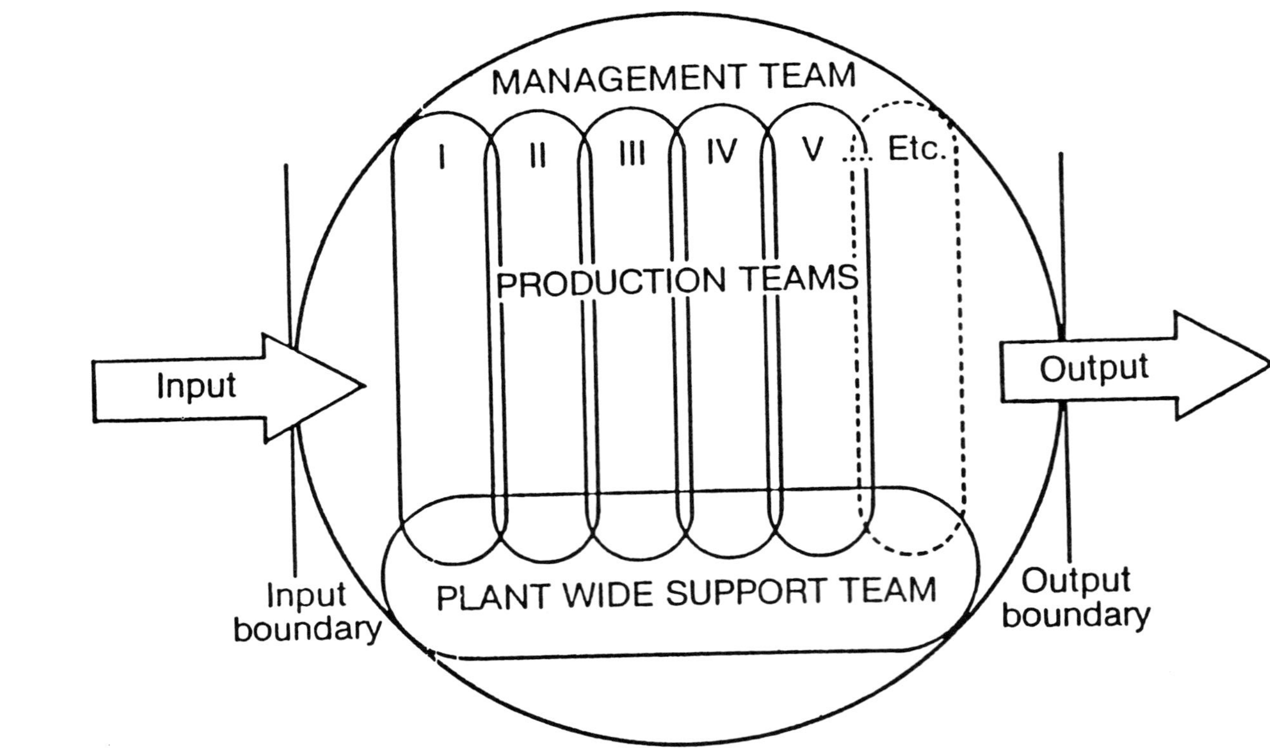

• presentation of STS proposals - May 1986

• first hirings - August 1986

• plant opening - November 1987

One of the key steps was the appointment of consultants to advise on all aspects of STS planning and the subsequent holding of a 'Search Conference'. This event was held 'off-site' and involved P&W Canada's top 30 executives in the definition of the value system they wanted for the new Halifax plant. This meeting gave endorsement and legitimacy to the development of the Halifax STS and provided a clear signal to P&W corporate employees that the new approach was supported at the most senior levels of the organisation.

The basic purpose of the 'Search Conference', as one P&W employee put it ,was to "empower the people". In the light of this, in August 1986, the plant manager was 'empowered' to recruit his own core group of managers and operators. Only four of the new employees came with previous P&W experience, although there was no requirement to recruit outside P&W. In effect, the plant manager was mandated to recruit people to create a culture in the plant which would be free from any constraints of P&W traditions and established values.

Recruitment and training. Recruitment and training were regarded as key aspects of the creation of the new culture and an effective STS. The plant manager recruited a core group of 30 employees. This group was built around five managers who formed the management team and manufacturing and support teams (see below). The core group took ten months to build.

The recruitment process included the completion of detailed application forms, telephone conversations, project familiarisation, (it now includes a plant 'walk through' so that candidates become familiar with what goes on and how), and extensive interviews, including one with the plant manager. For technical staff, qualifications are "a must" - but social and interpersonal skills are regarded as pre-eminently important. It is characteristic of the thoroughness of the recruitment programme

that the plant manager and all of those involved in the process had themselves been trained in recruitment techniques beforehand.

The process was followed by an induction training programme for the new recruits. This included courses in time management, training in goal setting, a three day course on the STS and a one week programme entitled 'Engine Tear Down'. The purpose of the latter being to make clear to everyone (literally everyone) working in the plant the importance in the final product of the component parts produced by the plant.

Almost before the induction period was over new recruits sometimes found themselves participating in other training relating to the needs of the various jobs: possibly a technical awareness programme or training in the use of programmable logic controllers.

Organisational structure. The structure of the Halifax STS is quite unlike that of a conventionally organised plant. There are only three organisational levels: plant manager, individual managers and operators. Managers, however, are not seen as being there to manage, at least not in the conventional sense; they are enablers and facilitators. The structure is set out in Figure 1.

Teams and meetings. Halifax runs on a system of interlocking teams or "autonomous work groups". The teams are not chaired by the managers but by operators, on a rotating basis. A common question put by visitors to the plant is, "but who tells people what to do?" The answer is no one. The teams make their own decisions through consensus building. Individuals are "empowered" to contribute freely, to show initiative and to come up with ideas with no fear of being put down or stepping out of line. They are empowered to help their colleagues, to swap jobs within the team and to decide what training they need. All this is reinforced in the day-to-day cycle of team working, identifying problems and finding solutions.

Structurally, there are three teams covering management, manufacturing and support functions. Typically individuals will spend some time in the support team if they are mainly concerned with production and vice versa. As an example, a 23 year old female graduate chemical engineer working as a production operator will spend time in "shipping and receiving" so as to be able to provide back-up to that team should the need arise. The same person could well be on the 'pay' team looking at the compensation package as well as on other teams considering other matters. To casual observers (unless they came from Japan) there would seem to be a proliferation of meetings, some of which end inconclusively because no decision has been reached. Much of this would cause the greatest exasperation to the manager of a conventionally run business.

The business process is surveyed each week at a roughly one hour general assembly of all employees, chaired in rotation by members of the management team. The plant manager makes his report as does anyone else who has any matter to raise. The agenda is open, drafted by a manager and pinned on the notice board to enable any member of the plant to add any item they think should be included. This again empowers people to contribute.

Reinforcement

There is a danger that the Halifax STS may regress into a conventional structure, particularly if individual managers, and especially the plant manager, begin to exercise status-based assertiveness. The combination of meetings, their structure and organisational mix are designed to make this regression as difficult as possible. Other measures mentioned below also reinforce the system.

The benefit system. Every employee is salaried. All have the same holiday entitlement. There are no 'perks'. It is said that "there is only one perk and that is an office without a door". There are no company cars, no reserved parking, no personal secretaries. If a manager needs a new light bulb he or she will change it. Everyone cleans their own desks or workspace and moves their own desks if the need arises. There is no 'clocking on'; everyone is on their honour. This reliance on peer pressure typifies the Halifax approach to the operation of its STS.

Pay. There are no job specifications or grades. Employees are paid on the basis of their skills. The pay curve is somewhat different for the management and support teams but that for those in the manufacturing teams rewards early skill achievement. The curve rises quickly in the early stages and flattens out as the total skill framework is covered. Consequently, the impetus to take personal initiatives in the acquisition of skills is reinforced. The system has the added advantage of rewarding seniority in attainment and not seniority in years.

Appraisal. Individuals appraise themselves and then share their appraisal with their team members before discussing their appraisal with two members of the management team. Appraisals, which were carried out annually, but were then changed to six monthly intervals, and were subsequently planned to move to a two month cycle, and were designed to focus on training needs. Appraisals are seen to be the key to skills attainment and hence increased pay. Appraisals cover the quality of an individual's work, their output, job knowledge, use of worktime, planning capabilities, their co-operativeness and work commitment and their ability to meet objectives and show leadership. However, the essence of the process is not to measure people but to identify remedial training requirements.

Communications. Day to day meetings persistently reinforce cultural values and the creation of an open society of individuals and equals. The exchange of information is considerable and includes the circulation to employees of what would in other circumstances be considered confidential. People are trusted. Decisions cannot be taken without appropriate knowledge and, as the plant functions through teams and non-managerial decision taking, the teams have to be kept informed.

The communication process is seen to be very important. Considerable emphasis is placed on achieving a high quality of presentation. The general meeting room contains $50,000 (Canadian) worth of equipment to achieve this. Notes of meetings are made on a flip chart, entered into a word processor and circulated within minutes of a meeting's conclusion. Electronic mail around the plant ensures fast and wide circulation. Meetings are held at a round table to emphasise that everyone has an equal part to play.

Training. Training for skills acquisition co-ordinates with the reward system. As well as induction training, the orientation programme on the Halifax STS and the 'Engine Tear Down' course, considerable effort is put into training for job rotation. The aim is to develop employ-ees to the point where they see themselves as engine makers, rather than as machinists or electricians or having other specific job functions. Training for satisfactory job rotation is designed to be completed over a period of one and a half years.

Participation. The 'empowering' process has helped identify problems and create solutions more quickly, and with more technical coher-ence, than is often possible through the usual corporate channels. The expectation that spontaneous contributions will be made by all employees has cut the problem solving time cycle considerably. Software problems, which would normally have been referred to P&W's Corporate Systems facilities, have been solved within the plant.

Interface problems

Apart from the challenge of setting up and making the system effective within the plant, problems have occurred at the corporate/plant interface. P&W Canada corporate staff were particularly heavily involved in designing the technological aspects of the plant. The social system within the Halifax Plant was developed later. It is said that the Japanese make their plant designers the implementers. This was not the approach P&W used and it is thought that the Japanese approach could be more effective. Some employees believe that 'ownership', which is important in the 'empowering' process, has been lost to some extent because the implementers were not involved in the design stage.

A further problem at the corporate plant con-cerns communications. Typically, 'corporate personnel' speak to 'plant personnel', and 'corporate engineering' to 'plant engineering'.

In a plant that uses no functional titles this creates communication difficulties. As a result Halifax has had to create job titles, such as Quality Assurance Manager, to enable the corporate/plant interfacing to work smoothly. The reality is that the Quality Assurance Manager in Halifax is the manager of information systems.

Suppliers, too, have problems. For the most part conventionally structured themselves, they find it difficult to relate to an organisation in which no one is specifically identified as the purchasing manager. Relations between plant and supplier can be made more difficult when key purchasing decisions are made at corporate level, for instance in relation to software, while the implementation process is left to the plant.

Other problems are of a less strategic nature, though they could have accumulative impact on the progress of the project. The pressures of work make it difficult to create time for train-ing. Also the pressures on management were so great in the start-up that finding time for management training was a particular problem. Meetings were very demanding on people's time and the time for meetings had to be set against exacting schedules for completion. A further problem found during the establishment of a structure of work designed to maximise the intellectual input of employees, was that for some people acting on their own proved very demanding and seemed a heavy burden at first.

Results

One benefit is the commitment, openness and applied technological competence of the plant's employees, whose average age is only 25 years. Problems are identified and exposed very quickly. They are often handled systematically at source or communicated rapidly to those who can solve them. The speed with which problems are handled and resolved is an important benefit which is expected to have a telling effect on the underlying rate of, and potential for, productivity growth and product quality.

It is too early to make judgements about the financial performance of the Halifax plant. It

has to be remembered that P&W are looking for
long term benefits. Nevertheless the aim of
reducing quality deviations to 1 per cent of that
of a conventional plant, just one of the objectives of Halifax, would appear to be extremely
difficult to achieve in circumstances other than
those at Halifax. P&W have come to the
conclusion that such targets are probably unre-
alisable in a conventionally organised plant. To
that extent Halifax does seem to be proving the
potential of a new approach involving the use
of advanced technology, computerised systems
and new working practices.

Some lessons

A general lesson emerging from Halifax relates
to the issue of computer-integration. Integration is not confined to the plant; integration
reaches down into suppliers, into customers
and into headquarters. All aspects of this need
to be appreciated before making such investments.

Perhaps the most important lesson of all, on
which everyone in the Halifax plant is agreed,
is that the vastly complex high-tech computer
integrated factory - 'tomorrow' for most companies but 'today' for P&W - can only be successfully operated through appropriate working
practices. These require that everyone is
accorded the same level of trust and respect.
Otherwise the investment will not realise its full
potential.

Another important lesson, related to that above,
is that a well educated, technically qualified
workforce is essential, and its capabilities must
be underpinned by continuing training. Training has been a key element in ensuring effective
job rotation, essential for the achievement of
very high levels of individual flexibility and of
team working.

The final lesson for other companies is not that
Halifax will achieve new levels of productivity,
quality, product reliability and technical
sophistication but that in doing so it will be
establishing a new industrial model capable of
competing with the best in the world well into
the 21st century.

REUTERS HOLDINGS

THE THREAT TO AN ESTABLISHED CULTURE

There are some 160,000 Reuters Screens around the world, conveying financial and company information in real-time mode twenty four hours a day. Reuters is the epitome of the global information organisation.

Reuters began as a news agency 137 years ago and developed a well defined culture which continued to the beginning of the 1980s. Since it went public in 1984 the company has grown considerably and made £109.6 million profit on a turnover of £866 million in 1987. Reuters has absorbed 10 major acquisitions in the space of four years and increased the number of employees threefold to 11,000. The question facing Reuters, having come so far is "whether the culture which helped make Reuters will ensure its survival and continuing growth into the future". The case study describes some of the implications of change for Reuters culture.

Background

Founded in 1851, Reuters became a public company in 1984. With its HQ in Fleet Street, the company is organised into four geographical areas: Europe (generating 56 per cent of revenue in 1987), Asia (21 per cent), North America (21 per cent) and 'overseas' (4 per cent). It is a transnational organisation, both by location, (it maintains offices in 171 cities in 80 countries), and by philosophy (its share structure has been designed to guarantee that Reuters should never pass into the hands of any one interest group or faction, and that its traditional commitment to integrity, independence and freedom from bias should be preserved).

Reuters is the world's leading news organisation and supplier of information services, serving business clients in around 115 countries, and media clients in nearly 160. It obtains its business data from over 150 exchanges and over-the-counter markets, from data contributed by some 3,500 subscribers in 79 countries, and other news from a world-wide network of almost 1200 journalists. It distributes the information via over 160,000 video terminals and around 4,600 teleprinters, and directly into clients' own computers.

While Reuters may be associated in the public's perception with journalism and media services (including general and economic news and news pictures), in fact sales to the media market account for a diminishing share of revenue: 7 per cent in 1987, as against 55 per cent earned by money-market information services transmitted through a computer-based network.

Most business subscribers, in around 24,000 locations throughout the world, receive Reuters services through the Reuter Monitor System, based on the world's largest privately-leased communications network. Using a keyboard and a video screen, subscribers can access real-time news and price information covering markets for money, commodities, equities, bonds, shipping and energy. Historical databases on money are also available, together with products which enable subscribers to analyse, summarise and reformat information.

The same network provides facilities for dealing in currencies, bonds and bullion between subscribers. Shares can also be traded electronically through a system operated by Instinet, a Reuters subsidiary. Finally, Reuters offers a range of interface systems for individually-designed dealing rooms, mostly built by a US subsidiary company.

Reuters information packages thus unite real-time news and prices with high-speed dealing communications, data processing facilities, graphic displays and archival information. While the company has significant competitors in many of these individual markets, its unique strength lies in its ability to generate and deliver a total information package. Clearly, computing and communications technology are at the heart of Reuters information services.

At the end of 1980, Reuters employed less than 2,900 people world-wide. By March, 1988, Reuters employed almost 10,000, fewer than 2,800 of them in the UK, including HQ staff. As Figure 1 shows, only about one in every eight is employed as a journalist. Reuters employs almost as many computer operators, programmers and analysts as journalists, and nearly twice as many engineers and technicians.

FIGURE 1:

OCCUPATIONS IN REUTERS, MARCH 1988

Journalists	1173
Technical	4196
Sales executives	669
Accounting	802
General administration	1056
Others	1690
TOTAL	**9586**

This background information should help to provide an understanding of what the organisation is, and does, and help put into context Reuters "management of change" problems:

• it is not yet a large company in employment terms, but it is fast becoming one;

• it has developed from its base as a news media service, though this traditional base remains significant in itself, as the origin of the company's values or culture, and as a vital marketing aid to the sale of other computer-based services; and

• it is not a culturally British but a non-aligned, supranational company. As they say, "when you join Reuters, you leave your nationality behind".

The nature of change

Obviously, it is impossible to deal fully with a company of this complexity in a short case study. This study concentrates on how the UK staff of Reuters have been adjusting to recent change, and how they are preparing for the wider changes envisaged for the organisation as a whole by timely investment in the company's physical and human capital infrastructure.

Many case studies of successful "management of change", including some in this series, are about corporate rescues. They focus on how

organisations have introduced specific policy initiatives in response to the emergence of a threat to their ability to remain competitive in their traditional business activity, often in declining markets. The story has an identifiable beginning (the threat), a middle (the management process), and a quantifiably successful ending.

The Reuters situation is almost completely different. It is about managing continuous change in response to a variety of opportunities (in markets, products and technology) for developing different business activities, in order to sustain continuing growth and profitability. Like the management of change, it is a continuing story with no obvious beginning and end. Throughout the 1980s, the story has been one of successfully managing rapid growth. The goal for the 1990s is to sustain that growth.

The Background section has outlined what Reuters looks like now. The following sections will trace how it got there. They begin with a snapshot of what Reuters looked like in the mid-1960s. Next, key milestones in the 1970s and 1980s are identified, together with the kind of changes which needed to be managed. The final sections set out some of the policies introduced to strengthen Reuters capability to cope with change successfully.

The starting point: Reuters in the 1960s

Twenty years ago, Reuters was a markedly different organisation. For more than a century it had been a highly-respected member of the international wire-service news fraternity, producing up-to-the-minute dispatches on business and general news for the media markets (primarily newspapers) worldwide. Although it maintained a world-wide network in order to provide this service, it was financially not a very successful organisation. In 1964, Reuters made an after tax loss of £53,000 on a turnover of £3.5m. It was still a small company, employing only 1,350 people worldwide. Of these over 400 were journalists.

The contrast with today, in technology used, in product range, in markets served, in levels of profitability and in manpower levels is probably more stark for Reuters than for most other companies. A lot of change has clearly had to be managed. However, certain key strengths of the 'old' Reuters News Agency - the international network, the Reuters journalistic culture (based on such values as accuracy, objectivity and independence), and the associated rejection of nationalism - remain alive in the new, 'electronic publisher' Reuters.

The key changes

Technology. In 1964 Reuters made a technological breakthrough in pioneering the use of computers to transmit financial data internationally. They developed and marketed a stock market price quotation system - "Stockmaster" - capable of replacing ticker-tape machines. Reuters had long had a tradition as a user of the latest available technology, and of being pre-eminent in the dissemination of financial information. Probably the best-known example of this goes back to 1850 when the founder, Paul Julius Reuter, identified a niche in the market, in the form of a physical gap (between Brussels and Aachen) in the European telegraph network and used a flock of carrier pigeons "low band width analogue devices" to take stock market prices across it.

Stockmaster has been Reuters most significant technical innovation. The head of Reuters small new computer bureau, (now its MD) recognised that electronics provided a major opportunity. The technology could be used to transform the existing news wire networks into international networks for the instantaneous transmission of financial data.

Subsequent success of the product created a more general awareness that the company's future could be based on, and revolutionised by, the computerisation of its services. Computerisation also offered an opportunity to apply the technology to the development of a wide range of new products for new markets.

Products and markets. An important opportunity presented itself in 1971, with the ending of fixed-rate currency exchange controls (the Bretton Woods Agreement). Reuters recognised that banks and company finance managers would need instant information on rapidly-changing prices of currencies. The Reuter Monitor, launched in 1973 for that purpose, was Reuters major product innovation, a computer-based information network which provided for the first time a real-time data service on currency rates. It effectively created a market place for foreign exchange: an electronic information system giving currency dealers access, via Reuter-leased terminals, to foreign exchange quotations, recommendations and other information. The data was entered directly by other dealers and by Reuters own financial journalists, and distributed over high speed satellite and cable links. By the end of 1987 Reuters money services were being received in more than 110 countries.

The coverage of Monitor has subsequently been expanded to carry news as well as prices, and to cover securities, commodities and energy as well as money. Before computerisation, to quote one observer, "as far as markets were concerned, Reuters didn't exist". But since Monitor, a new phrase has come into circulation, "if you're not on the system, you're not in the market". There are competitors, but Reuters has retained the leading-edge position it gained by identifying a market need and moving quickly to satisfy it.

In 1981 the creation of a new product, the Reuter Monitor Dealing Service, marked a further large-step development of the company's networking services. In place of traditional trading by telephone and telex, perhaps on the basis of Monitor information, dealers were enabled to use the existing network to establish direct private trading contact with their international counterparts. By mid-1988 the service was handling 735,000 conversations a week between around 6,000 dealers with possibly 30 per cent to 40 per cent of worldwide currency transactions going through the system. The new service signalled a move, not untypical of information companies, from providing information to providing transaction handling. It actually created a formal exchange for foreign currency, since previously none had existed.

The significance of these two applications of new technology for the present and future management of change is considerable. Together, they now account for over half of Reuters' revenue. By their success, in less than a decade they effectively made Reuters into a different company. While it still offers a worldwide news wire service, and actually employs twice as many journalists as in 1981, the company has also become a real-time transactions processing centre for world currency trading.

By enabling the network to attract the critical mass of traders necessary to make electronic trading feasible, Reuters has created a basis for many possible options for future product development. The Reuter Monitor Dealing System itself is being upgraded to provide fully automated trading in 1989. Reuters is co-operating with the Chicago Mercantile Exchange to provide an electronic out-of-market hours dealing system for futures traders. Volume on the Instinet share trading system has risen to new records.

Organisation. Between 1980 and 1984, the number of installed terminals and total company revenue grew fast (by about 350 per cent). Employment grew by 35 per cent, and profits by 2,000 per cent. The growth made possible the flotation of Reuters as a public company in mid-1984, which in turn generated £52m of new capital to finance future growth to strengthen its leading position in integrated information services.

Over the next 3 years Reuters acquired 10 related companies in Canada, the USA and the UK in order to enhance its technological, product and market strengths in all three of its major product areas: media services, financial services and client systems. Together with organic growth, these acquisitions increased earnings, pre-tax profit and employment, all by roughly 250 per cent.

Strategy. The main elements of the company's published strategy are:

• expand global databases of real-time and historical news and information, through internal development and acquisitions;

• maintain a world-wide network of quality, by research and development and investment in the network infrastructure;

• expand the communications, dealing and automated trading facilities offered to subscribers, on both a worldwide and a market basis;

• broaden the flow of new products and product enhancements, particularly for the purpose of data manipulation; and

• provide integrated packages of information and communications products and services.

The change management task

Despite the stock market crash of 19 October, 1987 (the development of which was tracked by thousands of Reuter screens) the aim remains one of transforming the company into a "one stop shopping" global information supermarket for the financial services industry. It recognises that the potential for long-term growth remains intact, as the financial world has barely begun to conduct business electronically. The components will be more new markets, new products, new services to existing clients, including the extension of the dealing system to everything from Government securities to futures. Reuters internal annual growth rate target for management purposes remains 25 per cent for pre-tax profits and for revenue over the longer term. One commentator describes the strategy as "slowing down to a gallop".

As the Wall Street Transcript of 21 December 1987 noted: "The ability to balance, co-ordinate and control that kind of growth is a very unique feat". In support of the strategy, Reuters recognise that they have to continue to invest heavily in research and development, particularly in the network infrastructure. They doubled spending on technical development in 1987 to £47.8m. Their new Technical Centre was due to open in London in 1989.

Delivering the strategy successfully will call for a wide range of solutions to hardware, software and communications challenges. These will include such developments as:

• continuing the expansion of the network, simply to accommodate the rising numbers of subscribers and increased traffic loading for existing services;

• upgrading and expanding the network in the longer term, to cope with new products and services;

• expanding the recently-introduced Integrated Data Network, which permits the fast packaging of a wide variety of products without the need for separate communications circuits, terminals and software developments;

• rationalising the products and technologies of the diverse technological groups which have recently been acquired by Reuters;

• continuing to make the presentation of data on terminals easier for the user, for example by split screens and providing search for information facilities by using key words.

Success in tackling these technical demands will place more demands on the other key infrastructure investment in human resources. What Reuter managers are clear about is that the ability to meet strategic goals will not simply be a function of how successfully they manage the technology. The business is not technology-led, but market-led. It is not concerned to advance technology but to apply it; albeit to state-of-the-art levels of sophistication.

As Reuters have found throughout the 1980s, bottlenecks to growth are more likely to arise from manpower problems than from problems with the technology. As systems become more complicated, their development time grows longer and the window of opportunity gets smaller. In this situation, it is crucial to get things right first time. That puts the priority on managing the associated manpower changes.

As Reuters experience since 1980 has demonstrated, there will be many such changes as the company grows and changes shape to accommodate the business strategy. While much of the recent employment growth has been through acquisition, growth has been significant in the 'core' organisation. In the four

years before Reuters became a public company (1980-84), employment increased by more than 30 per cent. While Reuters has not experienced major recruitment difficulties, such fast growth does pose management problems.

But the organisation is also changing its occupational shape, under the impact of its technology. In 1980, it still had only 400 staff world-wide classed as "technicians", (14 per cent of the total); as the earlier table showed, this group now exceeds 4,000 (44 per cent). In 1980 there were fewer than 100 "sales executives" (3 per cent of employees); now there are almost 700 (7 per cent).

Similar changes have taken place within the UK section of Reuters since the end of the 1970s. Three examples may be given from the "technical" functions. The number of Field Group installation and maintenance staff has increased from 10 to over 300. Whereas there was only a handful of programmers and systems analysts in the early days of computerisation, today there are 250. Press telegraphists who numbered 180, the embodiment of the 'old' technology, have been reduced to six. Many press telegraphists, were retrained as computer programmers or operators. Some of the fast-growing Field Group were teleprinter mechanics who had been retrained.

In addition, the tasks which people have to perform within apparently unchanging functional titles have changed dramatically, as process technology has changed. Reuters clerical and secretarial staff tasks have changed just like everybody else's. But the jobs of some other grades have changed no less, with editing journalists being a key example. London is the editorial heart of the company, where about 60 per cent of all editorial staff are still employed. Until 1980, their work was on a traditional hard-copy basis. Then, editing on VDU screens was introduced, involving some retraining. 1986 saw the advent of a new, highly-sophisticated video editing system, requiring a major retraining effort. The job today bears no relation to the editorial job of 1980.

The response - towards a people strategy

Reuters expects these technology-driven trends to continue into the strategy period. Some quite new skills will be required, such as staff who understand both computing and communications technologies. Conversely, some old skills will become obsolete as certain products decline. Some groups will increase relatively and often absolutely; for example those with marketing and software skills and experts in handling databases. Other skills which will decline include hardware skills, as the technology makes installation more customer-friendly, and routine clerical skills. Other standard occupational labels will conceal very different skills; for example, salesmen will increasingly need both a sound technical background and wider understanding of products and markets.

Many of the manpower changes listed above arise on a day-to-day basis. Responding to operational needs and solving problems is a major (and enervating) task for Reuter managers. As one noted "coping with fast growth is one of the more attractive management challenges. But that doesn't make it any easier". It would be possible to report many specific examples of successful responses, not least in the industrial relations field. (Reuters is one of the few "Fleet Street" organisations still operating in Fleet Street, apparently with excellent relations with trade unions).

However, this report concentrates on the company's recent growing recognition of the need for, and development of, a more strategic approach to manpower issues. It is possible to identify three main 'legs' of this approach. In order of priority these are management development, training more generally, and communications. The following discussion concentrates heavily on the UK operations.

Management development. Reuters fast UK growth from the late 1970s exposed some middle-management short-comings. "Like many companies, we didn't always pay enough attention to our management strengths in the past. The consequence was, we lost some

market opportunities". To minimise the chance of future lost opportunities, several initiatives have been taken. These are broadly designed to meet two needs: buying good people in the organisation and developing existing employees.

Importing outsiders. As is noted below, for historical reasons Reuters has a strong journalistic culture. One consequence is that many top managers are former journalists. Reuters recognises that there is no reason to suppose that good journalists will necessarily become people capable of managing a transnational electronic information company.

Therefore, more specialist managers with a good track record in helping other companies to manage change are being brought into the organisation to deepen its professionalism. A good example of this 'professionalisation' has been the staffing of the Personnel and Industrial Relations function, identified as central to Reuters' long-term objectives.

Introducing MBAs. Pursuing the theme of long-term "professional deepening" the company has begun to recruit Masters of Business Administration. In 1987, the first group (of 17) was recruited from leading educational institutions in the USA and in Europe. This is planned to become an annual input (to Reuters worldwide).

Graduate recruitment. The company now recruits (in the UK) 30 graduate trainees each year. They reflect the existing and projected changing mix of disciplines, so journalist entrants are not predominant. However, with some obvious exceptions (eg hardware engineers) the selection criteria pay relatively little attention to degree specialism, and lay more emphasis on linguistic fluency, numerical reasoning, verbal reasoning and all-round ability to communicate, because "people who cannot communicate will not go far in this organisation".

Performance appraisal has been introduced. As in many organisations, identification of, and attention to, top managerial capability has worked extremely well at the very top, but fit fully at lower levels. Reflecting the need for a

REUTERS FIGURE 2:

REUTER/IMI INTERNATIONAL MANAGEMENT DEVELOPMENT PROGRAMME

TIME	MONDAY	TUESDAY	WEDNESDAY	THURSDAY	FRIDAY
08.30	NEGOTIATION	NEGOTIATION	NEGOTIATION	NEGOTIATION	NEGOTIATION
	- Common assumptions about roles, goals, and standard moves - Defining "SUCCESS" in negotiation	- Building concensus - The effect of partisan loan perceptions - Tools for maximising influence	How the mind takes in information, how to communicate better	Motivation	Overcoming resistance
11.00 BREAK	- Long-range vs short-range objectives	- Intra-group process and multi-party dynamics	Renato TAGIURI		
10.30	- Group decision making and team dynamics - Role of trust and relationship in negotiation	- Mediation techniques for for negotiations and and managers	DEALING WITH INDIVIDUAL BEHAVIOUR	GUIDING BEHAVIOUR Reward Systems and other Levers	DELEGATION Concepts, Elements, Phases and Sources of Failure
12.00	Mark GORDON	Mark GORDON	Renato TAGIURI	Renato TAGIURI	Renator TAGIURI
	LUNCH	LUNCH	LUNCH	LUNCH	LUNCH
14.00	- Cooperative vs competitive approaches to problem - The power of legitimacy and objective criteria - The effect of walk-away alternatives - Distinguishing interests from positions	- Turning confrontation into joint problem solving - Application of theory to Reuters' practice - Choosing a system of negotiation - Changing the game: the other side plays	13.00 MARKETING CONCEPTS AND TRENDS - Positioning strategy - The market mix - Analysing demand and competitors	13.00 - STRESS MANAGEMENT - Definitions and concepts - Sources of stress - Identification - Interpersonal conflicts - Methods to combat stress	PERFORMANCE AND APPRAISAL EFFECTIVE MANAGEMENT OF PEOPLE Renato TAGIURI 16.00
15.30 BREAK	- Brainstorming creative options for mutual gain	- How to utilise and enhance negotiation power			16.30 - LIFE COAL AND CAREER PLANNING Tex SMILEY
18.00	Mark GORDON	Mark GORDON	Sandra VAN DER HERWE	Robert SHARPE	18.00
20.30 22.00	GROUP WORK	GROUP WORK	GROUP WORK	GROUP WORK & COURSE APPRAISAL	SYNTHESIS AND FEEDBACK Vijay JOLLY, Alden LANK & Ken JONES END OF COURSE DINNER

more coherent approach to development, performance appraisal is now taken very seriously and conducted systematically. Particular attention is now paid not just to the "top 6", but to the potential of 600 senior staff (world-wide), and to satisfying their personal development needs. Appraisal for all staff will become mandatory in 1989.

Placement is increasingly used to help satisfy personal development needs. In the past the importance of manpower planning and career planning has been well understood: "we had no trouble deciding what was needed. But doing something about it isn't so simple". Moving people around the organisation was made difficult by the geographically-scattered pattern of employment. Recent employment growth should somewhat ease those difficulties in the future, and create more opportunities.

Top management course. Ten years ago, top management training was virtually non-existent. Now it has become a Board-level agenda item. One outcome has been the introduction of a unique two-week Senior Management Course.

The decision to mount the programme was taken by the Board. Reuters chose IMI in Geneva (from among six top international establishments) because it had strengths which matched Reuters' emphasis on intellectual quality, internationalism and technical know-how. Reuters and IMI then jointly designed a course precisely tailored to the customer's needs. The faculty comes from seven different organisations, but their approach is closely co-ordinated by the IMI Course Director.

The course syllabus is attached (Figure 2). As one participant said "it tells you a great deal about Reuters". While not ignoring theory, it is clearly designed to enable participants to tackle practical problems. That intent is reinforced by the requirement that candidates should clearly establish their objectives before attending, have a debriefing session with their manager upon completion, and submit a report six months after the course on how they have been able to use their new knowledge.

Training strategy

The commitment of Reuters to this development is clear. Each course (for up to 35 students) costs over £100,000 in tuition fees alone. Over 200 managers are due to take the course. With the exception of the IMI course, it may be thought that none of the six management development initiatives is in itself in any way novel. But in total, they constitute a coherent, common sense, strategic thrust which would not have been present in the "old Reuters".

Before the introduction of management development much of Reuters' training was done "sitting next to Nellie". Reuters' explanations of why there is no option but to train is like that of many companies: "like many companies, we didn't do enough training in the past; we simply can't not do it now". In particular, the spate of recent acquisitions has thrown up training needs. However, their response has been strategic rather than simply reactive. Three aspects of it worth examination are targeting, benchmarking and the development of training facilities.

Targeting. Reuters has set itself a long-term target of allocating 1.5 per cent of revenue to formal, off-the-job training. In 1987, the actual spend was 0.6 per cent and planned to rise to 0.75 per cent in 1989. After the stock market crash, the company stopped all recruitment not directly aimed to produce revenue growth, froze top management salaries and called for cost reductions in some functions. By contrast, the aim to raise training spend by ten per cent in 1988 was restated by the Board. Top-level commitment is firm: "19 October will have no effect on training".

Benchmarking. Training decisions are mainly made by line managers. Managers frequently need guidance on deciding who needs how much of what kind of training. In an organisation as widely-dispersed as Reuters, on-the-spot professional advice may not be available.

REUTERS FIGURE 3:

REUTERS TRAINING REQUIREMENT GUIDELINES

The details below give an indication of how much time Reuter staff should spend on internal and external training courses each year. The main purpose of producing these guidelines is to assist the planning of future training requirements.

SALES		WEEKS PER YEAR
Sales Executives	- 1st Year	4
	- 2nd, 3rd Year	2
	- subsequent years	1
Sales support staff	- 1st Year	2
	- 2nd Year	1

MARKETING

Marketing Executives		2
Marketing support		1

TECHNICAL

Field	- 1st Year	4
	- subsequent years	2
Central	- 1st Year	4
	- subsequent years	2
Development		2

MANUFACTURING	2 days

EDITORIAL

Graduate trainees	10
Qualified (seniors)	1

FINANCE AND ADMINISTRATION

Accounts (UK)	3 minium (legislated)

SECRETARIAL AND CLERICAL

1st Year	1
Subsequent years	2 days

MANAGERS	1

GRADUATE TRAINESS OTHER THAN EDITORIALS

1st Year	6 weeks

Reuters have therefore issued guidelines or benchmarks to help managers to plan future training requirements. (see Figure 3). Even within the traditional, 'core' Reuters organisation, the changes in the occupational mix has raised question marks against the old journalistic culture, and offered plenty of potential for disharmony between, for instance, journalists, technical and sales staffs.

Reuters is one of those companies which regards its culture as important; though it tends to use the term "values" instead. Values such as accuracy, honesty, objectivity and independence have traditionally been so important to the success of the organisation that, while nobody has formulated them into a "mission statement", everybody knows and uses them. They constitute a major asset of the company.

Reuters hardly needs to be told of the contribution which such a "culture" can make to the coherence of the organisation and to its ability to manage change. Three principal changes have put the culture to the test in recent years. First, when Reuters became an electronic information company rather than a news agency in the 1970s. This raised questions about the journalistic culture's continuing relevance.

The second test came when Reuters became a public limited company in 1984. This prospect raised questions about the culture's continuing existence, and in particular whether the integrity of the news service might be jeopardised. So fundamental was this that the most senior executives had doubts about proceeding with the flotation. A solution was found in the protective device of the Reuters Founders Share Company Limited, which has duties (inter alia) to ensure that the integrity, independence and freedom from bias of Reuters shall at all times be fully preserved.

More recently, the acquisition of non-journalist companies has caused questions to be raised again about the appropriateness of the traditional values to the ability to weld disparate organisations into a single, integrated body with a shared purpose. It is feared that the Reuters culture could be diluted by growth. The Reuters case study cannot offer transferable solutions. All it can do is reaffirm from their experience the importance of a recognised and shared culture to the effectiveness of the organisation, and the importance of aligning management structures with culture in order to maximise that effectiveness. To the outsider, Reuters may seem to have an intellectual culture. The case study suggests that a characteristic of such organisations is that the people in them, however well-rewarded they might be, need to be able to influence the management of change, as well as be informed about it. Nobody knows that better than Reuters.

SCOTTISH STEEL AND TUBE WORKS, BRITISH STEEL

MANAGING TOTAL QUALITY

The Scottish Steel and Tube Works (SSTW) case study provides a striking example of the management of survival following an adverse swing in market conditions. SSTW, part of British Steel plc, make seamless steel tube, the bulk of which is sold to companies drilling for oil and gas in the North Sea. In 1985/86 oil prices fell to less than $10 a barrel, the exchange rate became disadvantageous and the demand for steel tube collapsed. The company moved from profit to loss and the factory faced the possibility of closure.

The case study sets out the survival plan and shows how this was linked to a scheme for Total Quality Management (TQM) designed to help bring about and consolidate attitudinal changes and new working practices.

Background

British Steel's recent recovery has been well documented. It is the product of a range of strategies, right across the company.

The Scottish Steel and Tube Works (SSTW) is a major part of the seamless tubes business and currently employs 2,000 people on two sites, at Clydesdale Works, Bellshill, (steelmaking and tube making) and six miles away at Imperial Works, Airdrie (finishing). SSTW is the biggest UK manufacturer, though relatively small in world market terms, of seamless carbon and alloy steel tubes, with an annual capacity approaching 200,000 tonnes.

Over 80 per cent of SSTW's employees are based at Clydesdale Works, which has two high-performance 80-tonne electric arc steel making furnaces, a continuous casting installation (a £22 million investment in 1984/85) two rotary forge tube mills, and a heat treatment facility. From here semi-finished tubes are transferred to Imperial Works, which has finishing facilities and a modern tube threading plant. SSTW has three main types of product, each produced in a wide variety of sizes and specifications as follows:

(i) Oil well casing. About 70 per cent of output. Most of it destined for major oil and natural gas extraction companies working on the UK Continental shelf;

(ii) Line pipe. About 10 per cent of output; for conveying oil and gas;

(iii) Commercial pipe. The remaining 20 per cent of output; for a wide range of applications; mainly sold to stockists.

SSTW's markets are highly cyclical. The casing market is especially volatile, with demand being closely related to oil prices. Customers' primary requirements are product quality, reliability and delivery on time. Demand is not especially price-sensitive.

As energy exploration extends to more marginal (and difficult) areas customers also demand a more sophisticated product. While SSTW is a major supplier to the North Sea, there is no shortage of other "local" higher-capacity competitors, notably in France, West Germany and Italy. Even the Japanese have shipped casing into the North Sea.

This is the underlying general context within which SSTW's 'management of change' programme was introduced.

Pressures for change, 1985

In the early 1980s, SSTW operated profitably. It benefited from three linked, externally-determined factors: its proximity to the booming North Sea market; the high price of oil; and an advantageous dollar exchange rate. With the price at $30 a barrel in the early 1980s, reasonable profits were achieved. In 1985/86, these advantageous factors changed abruptly. The price of oil fell below $10 a barrel. The exchange rate became disadvantageous. Customers virtually switched off demand for new exploration. SSTW moved from reasonable profits to large losses, and the factory faced the possibility of closure.

To survive, management saw that it would have to achieve radical improvements in its manufacturing cost base, in its product quality, and in its ability to deliver on time.

Two Responses, 1986/87

Management's response was a combination of short-term retrenchment policies which were mainly, but not simply, designed to deal with the immediate problem, and the development of more strategic proposals designed to put the plant, if it survived, in a better position to cope with unpredictable change in the future.

The first stage included a "Survival Plan Agreement", signed with the trade unions in April 1986, and the second was based on a "Total Quality Management" (TQM) initiative begun shortly thereafter. The primary focus of this case study is the TQM initiative. However, since TQM could not have succeeded in the situation which the Survival Plan Agreement was designed to correct, the agreement needs to be briefly summarised.

The Survival Plan Agreement

This Agreement summed up the severity of the problem facing SSTW:

• "There is an urgent need for all aspects of Works operations to be significantly improved, in order to reduce the cost base of the Works, in an attempt to achieve survival and restore customer confidence".

• "It is accepted that the reduction in unit costs through significant improvements in output, plant availability, yield, usage of energy and materials, and maintenance costs, together with manpower reductions and productivity improvements, are essential to the Works' survival".

Analysis by the management team, several of whom including the general manager (operations) were relatively new in post, revealed long-standing problems including poor manufacturing yields, indifferent product quality, excess manning, loose pay arrangements and inflexible working practices. The new manage-ment now had to achieve a sea change in desperate circumstances, and to do so quickly because "you can't jump across a chasm in two goes".

The Survival Plan Agreement accepted by the six signatory unions in 1986, tackled most of these problems and swept away an accumulation of well-entrenched inefficiencies. It reduced unit labour costs substantially. It was a difficult time, involving a major strike at the Clydesdale Works.

Management felt they had no option other than to face the strike if they were to have any chance of achieving their targets. "We knew a more positive management approach was wanted, and we had an idea what it would look like. But we had to sort out the basics first ...without the Survival Plan, we would have been closed down".

In retrospect "the basics" meant managers managing the business, employees accepting change as natural rather than something that had to be paid for and changing the culture in order to get everybody - managers and man-aged, steel plant and tube mills, production and support staff - pulling in the same direction.

The process was fundamentally about changing attitudes. The "more positive approach" to these aims took the form of the Total Quality Management (TQM) initiative. The Survival Plan's aim had been to restore basic competi-tiveness; the aim of TQM was to regain competitive advantage.

Total quality management

The general manager picked a small team of senior managers to map a way forward as part of British Steel's Total Quality and Performance (TQP) initiative. The frequency and expense of customer complaints, then averaging three per week, left the team in no doubt that SSTW had a serious quality problem. But there was no consensus about the solutions, because there were two views about the causes of the problem. The prevailing view was that poor quality was a technical problem, calling for technical solutions. As one participant said, "At that stage, I knew it was a 'people problem', but couldn't get them to see it".

TQM Phase I - Diagnosis and Preparation. Recognising the difficulty of being too close to the problem, the team invited external consultants to analyse it. This eventually came to be seen as Phase I of a four-stage TQM initiative. However, at that time (late-1986), on the basis of their interviews with managers, staff, shop floor employees, sales/commercial staff and key customers, and a broad analysis of the cost of quality, they saw the task as very daunting.

The picture was not entirely black. A review actually showed SSTW to have considerable inherent strengths, including:

• being a well-established company, operating in a specific market sector;

• having technically-qualified people who accepted the importance of quality, being close to the market and being the only UK supplier of such a wide range of seamless tube products.

However, these strengths were being dissipated by a wide range of cultural, organisational and attitudinal weaknesses identified by interviewees. One interviewee said, "the organisation structure hasn't changed with the market". Another said, "the plant is completely compartmentalised". Yet another interviewee said "there needed to be more awareness of customers". Further interviewees said, "we need to move from a tonnage mentality to a quality mentality". In short, the diagnosis was that the problem was primarily concerned with people.

The 'preparation' started from the top. In April 1987 the 12 most senior managers attended a 3-day residential Top Team Workshop in which consultants who had undertaken a diagnostic survey took them through the principles, techniques and programme of TQM. TQM was defined as "the route to continuously satisfying customer requirements at the lowest cost by harnessing everyone's commitment".

This had a major impact on some participants; as one departmental head noted; "for the first time, I realised that my department had customers". Most participants took longer to adjust to the new thinking. As one said; "we were all expert fire-fighters. Now we were being told our job was different".

TQM Phase II - Management Commitment and Focus. Top management chose to see the problems as opportunities for improvement and to commit SSTW to the full TQM Programme. This would be expensive and time-consuming but the aim was to recoup the direct costs "within a year". The consultants had argued (see Figure 1) that the increased cost of "preventive" investment in quality (eg training, TQM) would be more than repaid by consequential reductions in the costs of inspection and scrap.

But the initiative would only succeed if it had the commitment of the management team. As the operations manager observed, this could not be taken for granted: "quality assurance had always been at the bottom of the management meeting agenda. It now had to take priority over every other management task". As a beginning, it was moved to the top of the agenda, where it remains.

Gaining management commitment to quality assurance was seen to require a major training programme. This was based on a consultancy package, but with its content and methods tailored to meet SSTW's particular situation. The idea of manufacturing for quality and the use of techniques like fishbone analysis, brainstorming, teamwork, is not, of course, new. The TQM approach put all these techniques into a structured package which was introduced from the top. The approach was management led. Training started at the top and was cascaded down.

To ensure the programme's success and to demonstrate to all employees that management was taking TQM very seriously indeed, a senior line manager (who had been involved in the Top Team Workshop) was seconded as full-time TQM Programme Co-ordinator, and a steering group was set up to monitor practical TQM initiatives.

SCOTTISH STEEL: FIGURE 1

HOW COST OF QUALITY CAN BE REDUCED BY INTRODUCING T Q M

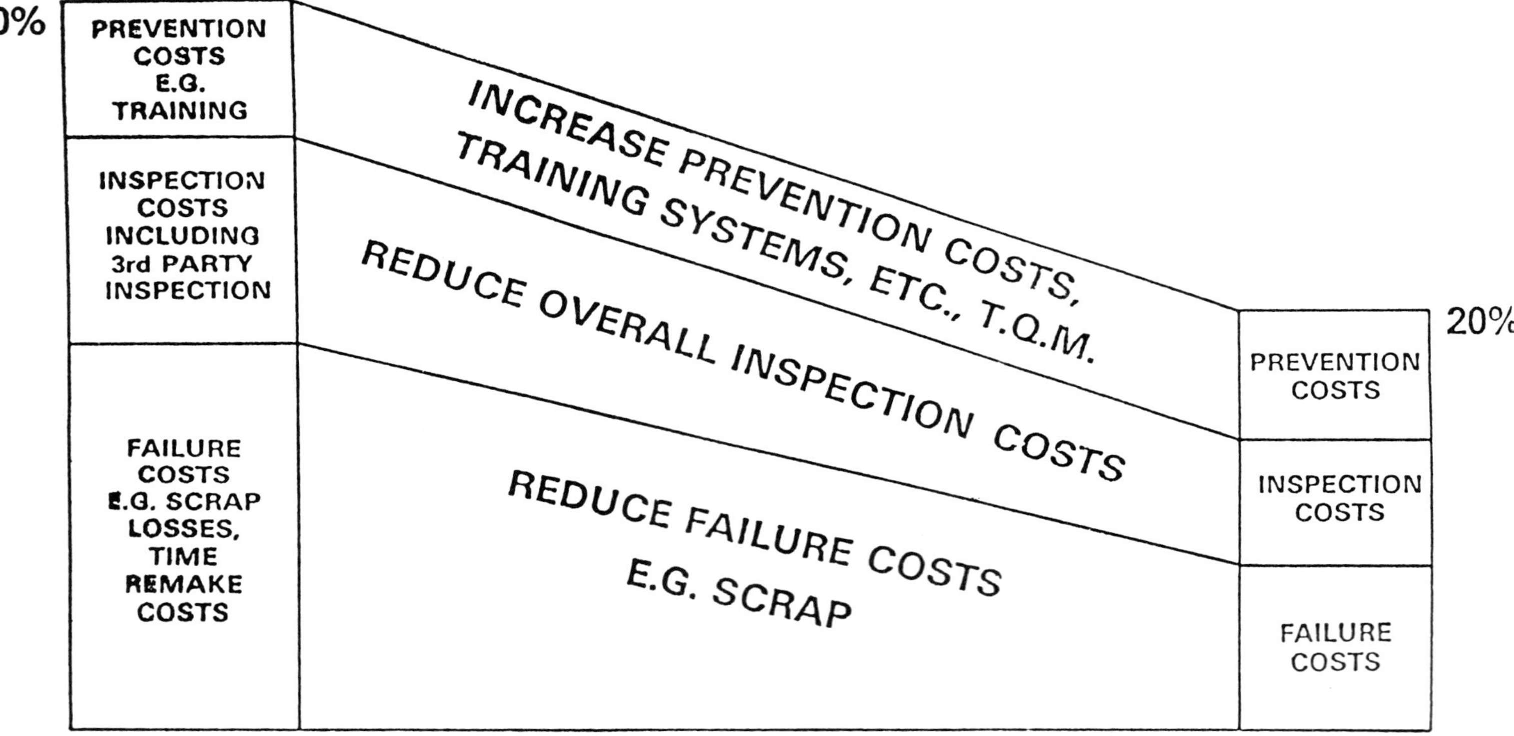

It was realised that careful choice of the co-ordinator would be essential. It needed someone from within the business, at a sufficient level of seniority; an enthusiast with a natural ability to communicate. The actual appointee came from the finishing plant, and was thus closer to the external customer than almost all of his colleagues. But as he himself observed, "every organisation has someone who knows about customers and is fanatical about quality".

Over the next two months, 44 more managers attended residential 2-day "Quality Colleges", designed to introduce them to, and gain their commitment to, the basic TQM principles (see Figure 2). The colleges were run by the consultants and the new TQM Co-ordinator.

Most participants felt that the principles were just "sound common sense", and some therefore found it too obvious. But as one put it, "it was so obvious, why did we need somebody to come in to spell it out to us?"

Another said, "but it made me start to think. Why, if our practices are so wrong. Are we just accepting them as normal? Why do we always blame the other guy for giving us problems? Why don't we spend more time asking the people actually doing the job, how we could do it better?"

While a small number of participants remained unconvinced, a quarter came away from the Quality Colleges fired with enthusiasm.

Clearly, to generate enthusiasm throughout the organisation would require considerable effort and resourcing. In July and August 1987, 14 middle managers who had attended the Quality Colleges were selected as part-time TQM Facilitators. Over the next year, their task would be to train the whole workforce in TQM.

The facilitators were deliberately selected from among 'the opinion formers' within the organisation. They were the kind of people who, especially in the new slimmed-down organisation, could not be spared from their jobs. None of them had significant or recent experience of training. Each received six days training in instructional techniques and in more detailed understanding of TQM. Some could not appreciate why they had been chosen, especially when they were thrown in at the deep end.

As one recalled "I thought, why am I here? I've never done any training. And how will I get my own job done with all this going on? Anyway, what has quality got to do with my job? That's how some of us were thinking then".

Some facilitators found it far from easy to become trainers, but following the one-week course, all 14 have operated successfully in practice.

TQM Phase III - Implementation. During the last four months of 1987, the new facilitators cascaded the TQM message further down through the organisation by mounting a 4-day, 8-module TQM training programme for 168 middle managers. In addition, the TQM Co-ordinator ran an abbreviated version of this programme for 24 of the managers who had been involved in the Workshop and Quality Colleges.

From this stage on, the training began to be linked directly into the business, in four ways:

• at the individual level, all trainees were asked to commit themselves to a Personal Action Plan, to be regularly reviewed;

• at the Departmental level, 30 Task Groups (inter-Departmental) and Action Teams (intra-Departmental) were set up, monitored by a Steering Group, to tackle key improvement opportunities. (Their results will be summarised later);

• at cross-Departmental level, reviews of internal customer/supplier networks were begun, on the principle that "everybody has a customer";

• at Business level a special news-sheet - "Quality Focus" - was introduced, designed to inform all employees about what TQM involves, and what successes were being achieved. So far, there have been five issues, supplemented in March 1988, by a dedicated "TQM Special Issue" of the SSTW Newspaper.

SCOTTISH STEEL FIGURE 2:

GUIDING PRINCIPLES OF

TOTAL QUALITY MANAGEMENT

APPROACH:	MANAGEMENT LED
SCOPE:	COMPANY-WIDE
THEME:	EVERYONE RESPONSIBLE
STYLE:	PREVENTION NOT DETECTION
STANDARD:	RIGHT FIRST TIME
MEASURE:	COSTS OF QUALITY

In the first quarter of 1988, full modular
training was also provided for 54 selected
white-collar staff, 66 senior manual grades, and
some trade union representatives.

By this time, the shop floor was saying "what
about us?" Finally, during March-September
1988, the Facilitators - this time assisted by
other managers - were providing 1-day TQM
Awareness seminars to all 1650 remaining staff
and manual employees, based on the modular
programme.

Tuition was provided in groups averaging 15
employees. Groups were mixed,by level, skill
and department, "to encourage the realisation
of what problems each may be causing for the
others". Attendance was mandatory, with each
trainee required to propose a simple Personal
Action Plan directly related to quality improvements to be achieved in his/her job.

A year on (July 1988), both facilitators and
managers assisting them were tired but
generally encouraged: "we think we've got the
message through to half of them".

In total, the four phases of TQM training
involved well over 3,000 trainee days, in about
200 training sessions. Including trainer inputs,
this approximated to 1 per cent of SSTW
employees' working time. This is additional to
training not directly related to TQM, for which
in the 1988/89 training year 20,000 trainee-days
been allocated. Excluding full-time trainees,
adult training/retraining accounts for over 2
per cent of working time. (A by-product of the
TQM initiative has been the realisation that
other forms of training need to be stepped up).

TQM Phase IV - Review and Relaunch. The
aim of the final Phase was to transfer
ownership of quality issues to managers. The
management team held a three day workshop
(August 1988) to review what TQM had
achieved, what actions needed to be taken to
maintain its impact following the highly-visible
training programme, and what lessons could be
learned about the management of change.

Achievements

Three years after the market collapsed, the
trading situation looked immeasurably better;.

SSTW did survive. It recovered its former
market share. Employment in 1988 was up by
200, compared to a year earlier. Unit labour
costs were reduced. Plant efficiencies did
increase.

The result of a review of customers (this time
by SSTW staff) was much more encouraging
than that conducted by consultants in 1986.
Customer complaints had fallen from 150 a year
to 23. Delivery on time performance had
improved substantially compared with the low
level in 1985/87.

Some major customers have even felt able to
reduce their (expensive) use of third-party on-
site inspectors. One has commented on SSTW;
"You must be delighted with the improvements
you have made". The unions have become
more involved. This would have seemed
unbelievable in 1986.

Some of the Task Groups/Action Teams have
clearly contributed to this revival, though not
all of them. SSTW will admit that some have
died, and the steering group will make use of
the lessons learned at the "relaunch" stage. Two
successes are particularly worthy of comment;
one at the beginning of the process (the melting
stage) and the other from the end (the finishing
stage).

In 1986, the ingot yield was 82 per cent. A
TQM task group identified a need for updating
training of the pit setters and teemers in operating procedures. In mid-1988, after the training,
the yield was 93 per cent. The financial savings
were substantial.

At the finishing end, a task group was set up to
improve the standard of pipe presentation to
customers. In 1986 the consultants' survey of
customers had reported that SSTW pipe was
immediately recognisable by its shoddy
appearance. In 1988, customers, frequently
comment on the excellence of presentation.

SCOTTISH STEEL: FIGURE 3:

SS & TW

TQM PROGRAMME EXPERIENCE

WHAT WE DID WELL/WHAT WE COULD HAVE DONE BETTER

WELL	WHAT WE WOULD CHANGE
STARTED AT THE TOP AND WORKED DOWN THROUGH THE ORGANISATION	ESTABLISHED MEASURED OBJECTIVES EARLIER (TOP TEAM WORKSHOP/QUALITY COLLEGES)
FIXED A PROGRAMME AND STUCK WITH IT	STARTED TASK GROUPS TOO EARLY WITHOUT PROVIDING GUIDANCE/TRAINING TO GROUP LEADERS
SELECTED THE RIGHT FACILITATORS AND TRAINED THEM WELL	
PLANNED FOR WHAT COULD/ MIGHT GO WRONG	ESTABLISH ORGANISATIONAL DISCIPLINE EARLY IN THE PROGRAMME
KEPT THE PROGRAMME WITHIN THE CONFINES OF SS & TW	TRAINING ROOM AND EQUIPMENT BARELY ADEQUATE
ACHIEVED EARLY SUCCESS TO BOOST MORALE	MODULE 5!
ESTABLISH AGREED GROUND RULES BEFORE STARTING TRAINING	

Progress has been made on the long list of "improvement opportunities" identified in 1986. In purely financial terms, SSTW reckons that the cost savings so far accruing from TQM have already more than met the costs of mounting it.

On a less measurable plane, there are several examples of how attitudes and approach have been influenced by TQM. Managers' answers to a simple "quality company" survey show a 'score' 50 per cent higher than a year ago. Managers at all levels now recognise that they have moved "from a tonnage mentality to a quality mentality". And change is beginning to happen outside the formal action teams. "People don't walk away from problems any more. They hold their own courts of inquiry".

Inter-departmental co-operation has improved and not just through the task groups. Support functions have been drawn into the process. An accountant said "we're much more involved now. This is no longer a 'back office" function. My colleagues and I are in the plant a third of our time".

General morale slowly picked up from the low point of 1986 and some part of this could be attributed to the involvement in TQM. Attitudes, of managers and managed, also improved slowly. But nobody expected progress to be anything but evolutionary because "you don't change a culture like this overnight; but we now recognise that that's exactly what we are trying to do"

Maintaining the Impact

To some extent, the future programme has already been mapped out. The planned Phase V foresees the continuation and extension of TQM. In particular they intend to:

• continue task groups and action teams;

• continue internal customer/supplier reviews, (because external customers' requirements for quality and delivery on time can only be if internal customer requirements are met);

• continue to develop personal measured performance in TQM;

• develop and extend communications, inside and outside SSTW;

• involve suppliers in the TQM programme.

This will need to be supplemented by a continuing training effort. SSTW have already reviewed this aspect. Their findings (see Figure 3) might help others contemplating a similar initiative. (NB "Module 5" is a heavily-statistical module, which facilitators found hard to get across to their trainees).

Managers recognise that the "total quality" concept has not yet achieved sufficient momentum to carry it along unaided. Even the successful ingot yield initiative suffered a temporary lapse when the pressure was relaxed. Not everybody, and that includes managers, is yet fully "on board". SSTW have learned a lot about training for TQM, but this highly-visible effort will be less needed in future; other means will need to be found.

It is recognised that the key management of change task will be to transform TQM, from being a novel and discrete activity into an on-going activity embedded in SSTW's every day approach to business. "TQM has to be seen not as a bolt-on extra, but more as the way SSTW does business".

Applying TQM Lessons to the Business

The TQM initiative has brought wider lessons for the business as a whole. The experiences of the past 18 months have shown that the new emphasis on "people solutions" (rather than technical solutions) has raised wider questions about the organisation's "people capability", which need attention if SSTW is to build on recent successes. In particular, managers recognise needs in the following areas.

Training. SSTW had a well established tradition of training activity. The TQM programme suggested a need both to increase this level of activity, and to re-focus it. As a result, the number of training instructors is to be doubled.

On-the-job induction training has been strengthened, not least because many of the TQM cost savings could be tracked back to training problems in the past.

More cross-disciplinary training has been required, including a specific emphasis on greater "commercial understanding" in all non-commercial (and especially production) areas. The task group approaches have highlighted a need for more emphasis on team working concepts. They also gave rise to another SSTW "golden rule"; 'Never assume that managers can run meetings; train them to do it'.

Communications. TQM has helped to forge informal internal communications networks where none previously existed; notably between departments (internal customers and suppliers). A news-sheet, called "Quality Focus", was also introduced, again where not much previously existed. The experience of TQM has re-taught everyone what they always knew but had forgotten: the importance of first-class communications. As one manager put it: "we now see improving the flow of information as synonymous with improving the product".

As with training, managers are now keen to make better communication an integral part of the SSTW scene, rather than a tacked-on support to TQM. To quote one middle manager whose department has been particularly successful in TQM work "communications remove people's fear of change". Since change had come to be recognised as inevitable and unpredictable, communications were seen to need to be professionally managed.

Personnel Policies. The TQM experience of asking individuals to set themselves personal action plans highlighted the need, as a senior manager observed "to encourage everybody to take initiatives, rather than waiting for someone to tell them what to do. We need to harness the brains and know-how of all our people".

Organisation Structure. Managers now appreciate that they face a particular difficulty in implementing a strategy for changing the SSTW culture. SSTW has, and will continue to have, three cultures: a steel making culture, a pipemaking culture, and a finishing culture.

The Task Groups and the TQM training programme have shown that it is possible to build bridges, at least temporarily, between these traditional islands of independence. It may be important to reinforce these bridges by organisational change, particularly when the TQM Co-ordinator role disappears.

Strategic Approach

TQM demonstrated to many managers the limitations of the "fire fighting" approach to the management of quality. It further showed the importance of being "outward looking", to customers and suppliers, both internal and external. Senior managers again translate the TQM experience into lessons for the business as a whole: that it must adopt a more outward-looking, strategic stance in order to manage future, unpredictable changes.

In a "slimline" organisation, change may mean making a commitment of time and resources. But again, TQM has taught SSTW that a competent management team will be prepared to make such a risk-investment, and get a return from it.

These are some of the major issues which the TQM experience has helped to illuminate. In tackling them, the management team will not forget some other lessons taught by experience, in particular the need to "sort out the basics first", "keep it simple; don't make the task too big to handle", "don't rush it; crawl, walk, then run", "tell people what you're doing; otherwise they will not be able to help you do it" and "use achievement measures that everybody can understand, so they can share in your success".

OLD MODEL	NEW MODEL
Labour specialisation	Multi-functional workers
Separation of brain power	Worker knows most about job
High quality = high cost	High quality = lowest TOTAL cost
Low cost = long runs and hard tooling	Low cost = small runs + flexible manufacturers systems
Value of inventory as buffer	Inventory is evil - hides problems
Economic order quantity	Acceptable quality level is zero defects
Optimise sub-systems	Optimise total system

WESTINGHOUSE ELECTRIC CORPORATION AND AEG-WESTINGHOUSE TRANSPORTATION SYSTEMS

CREATING A WORLD-CLASS ASSEMBLY OPERATION

At the beginning of the 1980s Westinghouse looked to computer-integrated systems to provide a competitive advantage in an increasingly constrained international market and an ever-more open and competitive domestic market.

The key element for Westinghouse's change programme was 'PMS' - Production Management System - a key module of which is MRPII, a computerised materials requirements programme. The case study pays special attention to the non-technical aspects of introducing PMS.

Background

Westinghouse is one of the world's largest corporations, employing 100,000 people in 26 business units operating in most countries of the world, producing a 1987 turnover of $11 billion (£6.5 million).

One of the smallest of the operating units with a turnover of $120 - $150 million is AEG-Westinghouse Transportation Systems, which was formerly known as Westinghouse Transportation Systems and Support Division. The unit employs 700 people in its non-unionised plant in West Mifflin, just outside Pittsburgh (Pennsylvania).

In September 1988, as a result of a joint venture agreement with AEG, which then became the majority partner, the Division ceased to be a wholly owned part of its parent company Westinghouse Electric Corporation. The events detailed in the case study refer to the period prior to the signing of this agreement and it is for this reason that AEG-Westinghouse Transportation Systems is referred to throughout the case study as Westinghouse.

Westinghouse designs and builds control systems for heavy and light rail vehicles, trolleybuses and "people-mover" systems. Its main transit products include propulsion and automatic train control equipment, while its people-mover systems are in use at airports and elsewhere. The Gatwick Terminal shuttle is an example of a Westinghouse project as is the Bay Area Rapid Transport System, 'Bart', in San Francisco.

The need for change

The study of change in any Westinghouse business inevitably involves an appreciation of the considerable corporate effort which helps support the change process in the individual units. Westinghouse Electric Corporation is constantly evaluating change needs. In the late 1970s and early 1980s, for example, Westinghouse's corporate development department staff identified fundamental changes in the pattern of international competition.

Markets were becoming increasingly global. The USA market, unlike a number of others, was comparatively open, with obvious implications for a number of Westinghouse units. Competitive pressures were by then increasing at a faster pace as market penetration by foreign firms grew. Issues of quality and delivery were becoming more important in meeting market needs. The increasing presence of Japanese competitors was particularly noticeable; their products being of very high quality and lower price to the customer in many instances.

Corporate Westinghouse took the view that, "the old industrial model of company operations based on more than 50 years of fine tuning of the early 20th Century ideas of Taylor, with functional specialisation, which Henry Ford, among others, had used to such advantage, was no match for the new industrial model that was emerging from Japan". The two models are contrasted by Westinghouse as shown in Figure 1.

It was against this background that Westinghouse Electric Corporation decided in 1981 to create a Productivity and Quality Centre (PQC) to provide central support for its units in their drive for improved competitive performance. Such was the importance attached to this development that they appointed a Vice President to head it up, with direct access to the Chairman.

The PQC provides a dazzling array of services and research papers, runs a considerable number of training programmes and has been involved in all the business units on an advisory or consultancy basis at one time or another. There is no problem for which the PQC does not seem to provide a telephone contact number, be it local area networks, factory automation software, Kanban, materials handling, statistical process control, value analysis, 'design for value' or even the management of change.

The PQC's role as a stimulator and as an agent of change has been very important to Westinghouse's development over the last seven years. The PQC has been extremely influential in forming opinions about the ways in which performance can be improved and in suggesting well researched solutions to a multitude of operational problems.

Consequently, change within Westinghouse itself has to be set in the context of Westinghouse opinion formed by the corporate level analysis of competitive trends and the conviction that only complete change to a 'new industrial model' approach would enable Westinghouse and its business units to succeed. Change, when it came to West Mifflin, was therefore planned as total change.

Westinghouse prospects

The West Mifflin plant was opened in 1975. West Mifflin and its other sister plant in East Pittsburgh were vertically integrated with foundries, manufacturing and machining capabilities and assembly operations. West Mifflin itself was involved in both manufacture and assembly and was run on conventional lines until 1982, when its change programme started. So, what was carried through was the total change of an established, relatively young, non-unionised plant. It should also be noted that at the time Westinghouse Electric Corporation as a whole was keen to see the outcome of the improvements. West Mifflin was something of a test-bed for possible approaches to the general problem of raising levels of productivity growth.

Prior to 1982, the signs of a declining market were apparent. While Westinghouse's market share grew somewhat, the total domestic market declined. The closed nature of many overseas markets made them extremely difficult to penetrate from an uncompetitive base. The issue, so far as the management of Westinghouse was concerned, was one of survival. This meant achieving new levels of quality, reliability and productivity performance.

Key elements of the change programme

Functional specialisation. Change was built around two basic decisions. One was to move all manufacturing operations from East Pittsburgh and concentrate them at West Mifflin. The other was to streamline, automate and computer-integrate the assembly and associated functions, such as inspection and inventory control at the West Mifflin plant. Westinghouse also increased its sourcing of parts and sub-assemblies from more suppliers.

At West Mifflin, the goal was to create a world class assembly facility, jumping in a two-year period from a classical machine shop to a fast-response assembly operation. This change was to be carried out at a time when the division was completing a record number of orders placed prior to the commencement of the change programme.

Operational discipline. In order to underpin the introduction and operation of the real time computer-integrated assembly operation, the West Mifflin management decided to introduce PMS (Production Management System). This Boeing developed system includes MRPII, a computer-based material requirements planning module.

PMS facilitates the computer-integration of production dependencies, through from purchasing, bills of materials, master schedule, production plan, shop floor control and inventory management to sales order administration and shipping. Its introduction forces recognition of the need for, and introduction of, operational discipline at every point in the plant.

The introduction of PMS requires major operational changes, entailing tough decisions and a demanding programme. That the West Mifflin plant introduced PMS, totally changed the plant, "everything except the four walls", and simultaneously met record production targets during the two year change period was acknowledged to be an extraordinary feat.

There is considerable pride in the result, at all levels, but the effort involved was considered to be enormous. "At one point I slept right through two days, I was so exhausted", said one manager. "There was a lot of hurt", said another.

Wider change considerations. In developing their strategic review prior to 1982 West Mifflin's management became increasingly conscious that a number of performance indicators needed to be greatly improved. "There was a pressing need to improve value to price and cost ratios" and it was emphasised that "waste represented failure". It was recognised that "error free performance should be the goal" and that "there must be a greater effort in bearing down on cost/time profiles".

It was also apparent that a number of organisational factors stood in the way of making these kinds of performance improvements. For example, manufacturing and assembly operations were the responsibility of separate departments and the resulting organisational barriers made it difficult to deal effectively with quality and delivery issues. Quality conformity and inspection was a tail-end and not a front-end operation, leading to unnecessary duplication of effort in rectifying errors. These problems were compounded by the fact that assemblers were unaware of the nature of the end product and sometimes compounded quality problems through ignorance. In addition, the organisation and layout of the plant (described as 'a bit of a mess') did not help the resolution of problems. It was against this background that Westinghouse took its decision to turn the plant into "a world class facility".

The process and results of change. How the change process was carried through is best considered in the context of some of the results which have been achieved in the period 1983 to 1986.

West Mifflin plant is now a model factory. It is clean, immaculately so, spacious, light, air conditioned and pleasant. There are carpets inassembly areas and plants around the walls. People are pleased they can wear decent clothes to work. Computer terminals abound; there are 700 terminals to 850 employees. These are the most obvious manifestations of the changes that have taken place.

The performance changes are no less impressive. Factory space of 125,000 sq ft in two plants is now down to 52,000 sq ft in one. Previously, two thirds of operating space was needed for inventory; now only 15 per cent is required. Output in the 1983 to 1986 period went up by 600 per cent, productive capacity by 400 per cent and productivity by 79 per cent. Material costs have been reduced by 15 per cent per annum. The compensation (ie wages and salaries) to sales ratio has fallen by 29 per cent and the ratio of quality costs to sales has fallen by 47 per cent.

In the target area of reduced cycle time major improvements have also been achieved. In 1983 the average product assembly cycle time was three months; it was reduced to one week. Considerable reductions in inventory and work in progress have been achieved, as have improved levels of inventory accuracy (parts are available when they are needed). These changes were essential to the effective operation of PMS. Inventory accuracy was at 60 per cent prior to the change but was improved to 98 per cent; 100 per cent is the stated aim. There is considerable pride in these achievements throughout the plant.

The change programme

Management decisions. The programme began in 1981 with offsite discussions among the senior managers about the need for change and the definition of the strategy. During this period a number of manifestations of management's wish to change were signalled to the workforce - reserved parking went and time clocks were removed (everyone was already a salaried employee). Importantly, management carried out an attitude survey to get every one involved and to help focus on performance issues. A wide range of consultations took place. "The majority of the suggestions came from the shop floor", one manager said.

In the first quarter of 1982 the decision was taken to begin the 'total change' programme. A specific manager was made responsible for the introduction of PMS and June 1984 was set for its full operation.

Organisational restructuring. Decisions were taken to adopt a computer-integrated division-wide system, based on the needs of PMS. This meant ceasing to do all computer work off-site, because turnround times would be too long and the costs too great for the new approach, which would change the system from manual batch to real time processing. The new system was to be 'organisationally seamless', with no functional separation of information. This in turn necessitated a change from the then functionally-oriented organisation to one based on product technologies. Five manufacturing groups were formed for motors and gears, power electronics, signal electronics, mechanical products and ILS (Integrated Logistics Support). These manufacturing groups were meshed together through the introduction of a matrix management structure.

Team working. The organisation's new focus was clearly centred on the customer. The engineering department was divided into teams which enabled them to co-ordinate their efforts with customer assembly teams which were set up when the new assembly process came into operation. Each order came to be processed as a programme with a designated programme manager co-ordinating activities with other departments and integrating the technology groups. The end result has been greater responsiveness to customer needs. The customers get to know their teams, have a specific point of contact with the company and know that their orders are being looked after in a special manner. The teams can follow work through as a total process, without the hindrance of the functional boundaries which existed previously.

Quality and suppliers. In order to reduce cycle times and raise overall efficiency the West Mifflin plant moved to pre-assembly inspection and quality control (in place of the rear end system which previously existed). A 100 per cent inspection programme was introduced to ensure that only perfect parts could be received by the assembly line and that defects would not cause production delays. This policy has had implications for Westinghouse suppliers, as some of the inspection is done at source. Also, suppliers are having to respond to time-adjustable delivery requirements as a result of the minimising of inventory levels. The relationships between the company and its suppliers have been made much tighter than they used to be. A computerised inspection control system has been used to ensure that any departures from specification would be taken up by the appropriate buyer with suppliers within 24 hours. 'Just in Time' did not immediately come to West Mifflin's suppliers but it was clearly on its way.

Assembly teams. The team concept has also applied to "kitters", the group of people responsible for bringing together inventory parts required in the assembly process. Under new arrangements, parts were brought together into product or sub-assembly kits for transfer by conveyor belt to the assemblers. Assemblers in their turn belonged to a flow line team, although each assembler worked on only one unit at a time and was responsible for its completion. Once again, the approach contrasts with that of the past.

Computer-generated discipline. Scheduling assembly was computerised, and all assembly operators were given a terminal at their workstations. They were given access to the system both to view production needs and draw up assembly reference material. Most employees could then carry out their own data entry in real time mode.

Assessing the changes. Clearly, the computerised discipline of the plant is one of the greatest contrasts with the past. Arriving at this level of computer capability has required a considerable amount of effort and reorganisation which should not be underestimated.

West Mifflin was fortunate in being able to rely on continuous advice from the PQC as well as on individuals with experience of introducing other PMS programmes. Not every company can do that, nor can they enjoy the corporate resources which Westinghouse places behind resolving technical, computing or other problems. Nevertheless, West Mifflin had to make things happen. They had to completely reorganise purchasing, manufacturing and engineering information, previously kept in three separate databases, into one database which was compatible with the needs of the real time computer-integrated system.

Managing these functional boundary changes was a much bigger task than it seems at first sight. Now, however, the company has a control system which integrates sales, purchasing, receiving, kitting, and assembly operations in real time mode. Storage and scheduling changes can be entered immediately, providing total visibility around the plant for any new requirements. In its totality the system is a powerful means of enabling resources and effort to be devoted to the key issues of customer needs and quality requirements.

Training for change

Management of change in a Westinghouse plant has the advantage of a "vast" underlying base of training activity. For instance, the manager of Information Management Systems, responsible for the introduction of PMS was a Bachelor of Science (Vocational Education and Science) and had received an average of three weeks training per annum, mostly in-house, for almost thirty years. In recent years this had included: training in computers, materials management, production inventory control and extensive training in management skills, including team working, 'numerous' courses in financial management and time management, among other IBM seminars, seminars on artificial intelligence and courses on managing change. Other managers had undergone a similar wealth of training. The result has been, not only the creation of high levels of management competence, but also the creation of an environment committed to training for change.

Training for PMS

Commitment to training, an integral part of the West Mifflin change programme, was centred on the introduction of PMS. At the outset, key people went to Boeing, the developers of PMS, for training in the system. Training films in PMS concepts were acquired for showing to managers and employees, so as to raise awareness levels. Lastly, a structured awareness training programme took all employees through all aspects of the PMS exercise.

An Awareness Training Programme began with a one day (8 hours) seminar for the General Manager, his immediate management team, other managers, professional staff and a number of key users.

This seminar was followed up with a further one day repeat presentation for line managers and their staff and yet a further seminar for support managers and their professional staff, including buyers and accountants. The result was that everyone was made aware of what was involved. The managers, who received three presentations, were fully conversant with PMS. This enabled management to play a full part in subsequently promoting wider awareness and explaining the new system. The seminars were later reinforced with a further four one day sessions. The awareness phase was seen as the easy part of the exercise.

Operational training in the use of the system was more difficult. A special training division was set up to handle this, with a small staff of professional trainers. The division was charged with developing a modular programme to embrace all the requirements of the PMS system. The 'Bill of Materials' module required 12 hours of training, 'Inventory Control' required 16 hours, 'Purchasing' required 16 hours. All provided a combination of hands-on experience and trial and error usage. In all, 75 per cent of employees were given operational training. Where they had no keyboard skills, appropriate training was also provided.

Functional training was also provided for managers and other employees affected by changes to the system. In groups of twelve, individuals from the engineering, drafting, purchasing and other functional parts of the organisation were taken through eight hour training sessions, to familiarise them with the operation and running of the integrated system and the PMS disciplines. It was mandatory for unit managers to be directly involved in all aspects of the training programme.

Organisational changes. The organisation was made flatter, the number of organisational levels was reduced and individual responsibilities became more broadly-based. With hindsight, it is acknowledged that even more training would have been desirable to enable people to cope more easily with their increased responsibilities. A particular reason for this was that the PMS system, once running, gave considerable visibility to all aspects of its operations and exposed operational mistakes almost immediately. The discipline of the system required immediate error correction, something which had not always happened in the past.

As the PMS programme moved from start-up in June 1982 to operational use in September 1984 the West Mifflin plant underwent, as has been mentioned earlier, major structural reorganisation as individuals moved from a system of individual to team responsibilities, involving product-based groups and customer teams. The enabling process for all of this involved a series of team building sessions. Several one day sessions were held for this purpose..

Without this intensive training effort it is extremely unlikely that PMS would have been up and running within what was seen to be a short space of time. Inevitably, the scale of the shift from the old system to the new created difficulties for many in visualising the nature of the outcome.

Customer and supplier implications. The implementation of PMS also had training implications for suppliers and customers. The new system and its implications were explained to suppliers through the buyers. It was later thought that this process should have been made more formal and should have involved them in in-house seminars, so that they could envisage the changes more clearly.

With the new system when Westinghouse buyers met with suppliers they had at their disposal a comprehensive computer-generated history of the suppliers' performance.

Customers too became involved, it is thought, with the changes being explained by the field sales force. Retrospectively a more formal programme, held on site, providing them with the total picture, would have been more effective.

Follow-up training. The amount of activity at all levels was described as "one hell of a training programme". One assembly worker said, "I get trained every day". The Training Division aimed to provide every employee with some 10 days training per annum.

The requirements were met by using the full extent of the computer and video network. Assembly workers, for example, could call up training modules on their personal terminals to take them through any assembly process with which they were having difficulty.

The initial training effort concentrated (necessarily) on procurement and manufacturing. Future productivity gains would, it was anticipated, be made in the pre-production stages, especially in design and engineering. New facilities, including engineering work stations with inbuilt simulation capabilities for design, would present new training needs.

Financial support. The introduction of PMS focused on assembly and related operations and did not directly involve changes in what came to be called the financial support department and accounting and financial control methods. A "21st Century accounting system" is seen to be an essential requirement for a plant run on a computer-integrated real time basis and for the introduction of PMS. It was recognised that the information database at the heart of PMS demanded consistent information covering all aspects of the business. In addition, the accounting practices needed to match and integrate with the computer system covering the rest of the plant. With hindsight, it is thought that all financial aspects should have been integrated into the 1982 change programme from the outset, so that financial and accounting personnel would have been part of the PMS planning team and fully involved in the implementation process.

West Mifflin developed a Financial Support Department, divided into three areas of responsibility, covering Financial Control, Financial Planning and Project and Corporate Accounting. Each of these was further sub-divided into teams; Project and Corporate Accounting, for example, had three teams.

The general aim was to improve service and to enable the teams to initiate ideas for improvements. This approach was seen to be dynamic and this image was reinforced by the setting up of what were referred to as "Travelin Teams". These went to their in-plant "customers" and did not wait to be called for.

The change of departmental title from Financial Control to Financial Support effectively marked an overall shift in philosophy. The department came to see its role as one of enabling and facilitating rather than policing, although the control aspects of its responsibilities had not been lost.

Some problems and possible lessons. Such has been the total transformation of the West Mifflin plant that it would be surprising if some problems had not arisen. In this respect the lessons for others would seem to be that the problems can be best handled if the management style is sensitive to the needs of people. As was said at the beginning, "there was a lot of hurt", the memory of which seems to have been long lasting. It is not possible to say whether this is a major issue for West Mifflin. It does, however, raise the point that if processes are made to appear to be more important to management than the people who run them, then the creation of model working conditions may not necessarily lead to the complete attitudinal changes required for sustained commitment to the new system. However, all those at West Mifflin were very proud of their achievements.

Another problem concerned the benefit system. In 1984 the plant moved to an 'All Merit' system based on an annual employee performance assessment which did not include any provision for the payment of costs of living or other general increases. The move to the 'All Merit' system involved the simplification of the grade structure, designating only five grades of shopfloor employees.

'All Merit' pay had a number of implications for operators. First, some employees moved from skilled manufacturing tasks to less skilled assembly tasks and suffered some loss of earnings. Second, a few other highly skilled workers found themselves at the top of the five grade structure, with no room for pay progression and no cost of living increases. Others found that progress through the tighter grade structure was not helped by the acquisition of new skills. This tended to undermine the strong Westinghouse tradition of actively encouraging its employees to voluntarily take up educational and training opportunities.

All these matters are under review. The lesson for others is that total change may need to anticipate possible anomalies in the reward system.

The future

The joint venture between Westinghouse and AEG of Germany seems likely to lead to further change and new opportunities for West Mifflin. While the joint venture is obviously designed to capitalise on the match of market strengths of the two companies - there is very little overlap - such a venture would have been unthinkable prior to September 1984. The venture has been made feasible by the change programme. Change at West Mifflin has been underscored by the clear recognition of the unrelenting pressure of market competition, so that "the goal is not to become, but to remain, a world class assembly operation". Or as one manager said, "you change or you go down the tube".